ECONOMIC AND SOCIAL COMMISSION FOR ASIA AND THE PACIFIC

STATISTICAL PROFILES   No. 14

WOMEN IN INDONESIA
A COUNTRY PROFILE

UNITED NATIONS
New York, 1998

ST/ESCAP/1767

UNITED NATIONS PUBLICATION
Sales No. E.98.II.F.63
Copyright © United Nations 1998
ISBN: 92-1-119849-6

The profile has been prepared under project BK-X20-3-214, on improving statistics on women in the ESCAP region.

FOREWORD

The call for the development of statistics and indicators on the situation of women has, for some time, been voiced in various global and regional forums. It was first recommended by the World Plan of Action for the Implementation of the Objectives of the International Women's Year, adopted in 1975. The recommendations of the World Plan of Action were reaffirmed and elaborated in the Programme of Action for the Second Half of the United Nations Decade for Women: Equality, Development and Peace. On various occasions, the Commission, stressing the importance of social and human development, has recognized the need for improved statistics and indicators on women. It has noted that better indicators are required to monitor the situation of women and to assess the effectiveness of strategies and programmes designed to address priority gender issues.

The secretariat initiated the project on improving statistics on women in the ESCAP region in 1994. The project aims to support governments in their efforts to promote the full integration of women in development and improve their status in line with the Nairobi Forward-looking Strategies for the Advancement of Women adopted in 1985. The project has been implemented by the Economic and Social Commission for Asia and the Pacific (ESCAP) through its subprogramme on statistics, with funding assistance from the Government of the Netherlands.

As a major component of its activities, the project commissioned experts from 19 countries in the region to prepare country profiles on the situation of women and men in the family, at work, and in public life, by analysing available statistical data and information. The profiles are intended to highlight the areas where action is needed, and to raise the consciousness of readers about issues concerning women and men. The 19 countries are Bangladesh, China, India, Indonesia, the Islamic Republic of Iran, Japan, Nepal, Pakistan, the Philippines, the Republic of Korea, Sri Lanka and Thailand in Asia; and Cook Islands, Fiji, Papua New Guinea, Samoa, Solomon Islands, Tonga and Vanuatu in the Pacific.

The secretariat hosted two meetings each in Asia and in the Pacific as part of the project activities. At the first meeting, the experts discussed and agreed on the structure, format and contents of the country profiles, based on guidelines prepared by the secretariat through Ms C.N. Ericta, consultant. The second meeting was a workshop to review the draft profiles. Participants in the workshop included the country experts and invited representatives from national statistical offices of Brunei Darussalam, Hong Kong, China, the Lao People's Democratic Republic, Mongolia and Viet Nam in Asia; of Marshall Islands, Tuvalu, and Vanuatu in the Pacific; and representatives of United Nations organizations, specialized agencies and international organizations.

The original draft of the present profile, *Women in Indonesia,* was prepared by Ms Evelyn Suleeman, at present Senior Associate, Insan Hitawasana Sejahtera, Social Science Research and Consultancy. It was technically edited and modified by the ESCAP secretariat with the assistance of Mr S. Selvaratnam, consultant. The profiles express the views of the authors and not necessarily those of the secretariat.

I wish to express my sincere appreciation to the Government of the Netherlands for its generous financial support, which enabled the secretariat to implement the project.

Adrianus Mooy
Executive Secretary

iii

CONTENTS

LIST OF TABLES

LIST OF TABLES *(continued)*

LIST OF FIGURES

LIST OF ANNEX TABLES

LIST OF ANNEX TABLES *(continued)*

PART I

DESCRIPTIVE ANALYSIS

INTRODUCTION

In Indonesia, social values and cultural traditions have by and large been favourable to the free and active participation of women in various spheres of everyday life. Unlike women in many other countries, Indonesian women have traditionally not been subjected to any rigid formalized discrimination in their family, social or economic life. The principle of equality between men and women is deeply ingrained in the State philosophy, *Pancasila* (the Five Basic Principles) and the 1945 Constitution, which guarantees equal rights and obligations in the fields of education, law, health, political participation and employment. The Agrarian Law of 1960 guarantees the right of women to own land.

A major achievement during the United Nations Decade for Women: Equality, Development and Peace was the inclusion of a special chapter on the role of women in nation-building in the Broad Guidelines of State Policies of 1978 and subsequently of 1983, 1988 and 1993. While declaring that "women as citizens as well as human resources for development have the same rights, responsibilities and opportunities as men in all aspects of civic life and development activities", the Guidelines also emphasize other basic concepts, such as woman's harmonious role in the family and society; respect for women's dignity; protection of women's specific biological characteristics/reproductive functions; and development of a favourable socio-cultural climate and enhancement of women's capabilities for wider participation in development.

In 1952, Indonesia ratified the United Nations Convention on the Political Rights of Women, under the terms of which women are ensured equal rights to employment, to vote, stand for election and hold public office. In 1980, Indonesia signed the Convention on the Elimination of All Forms of Discrimination Against Women and ratified it by passing Law No. 7 of 1984.

The endeavour to enhance the role of women in development has also been an integral part of national development. This is evidenced, among other things, by full recognition of women's issues as an integral part of the overall national development issues; the great importance accorded to the family as the basic social unit in society; and full awareness and recognition of the heterogeneous nature of Indonesian women and the need to develop a variety of programmes to meet the needs, concerns and aspirations of the different groups and strata.

The New Order Government has also demonstrated its commitment to the advancement of women through the creation of national mechanisms to facilitate women's participation in development. A semi-governmental organization, the National Commission on the Status of Women, was established in 1968 with the primary task of collecting data on the situation of women and making recommendations to the government. The Commission comprised representatives of women's organizations, and technical departments under a presidium or executive board of five elected members (three from women's organizations and two from technical departments). Committees, chaired by a presidium member, cover morals and religion; education and culture; health and social affairs; manpower and politics; and law and the family.

In 1978, an Associate Minister for the Role of Women was appointed to the Third Development Cabinet; this position was upgraded to State Minister in the Fourth Development Cabinet of 1983. Under the terms of Presidential Decree No. 25 of 1983, the functions of the State Ministry for the Role of Women are as follows:

(a) To prepare and plan the formulation of government policies pertaining to the enhancement of the role of women in all fields of development;

(b) To coordinate all activities in order to achieve cooperate, balanced and integrated efforts in overall implementation;

(c) To coordinate the operational activities of various government institutions and agencies concerning programmes on the enhancement of the role of women in all fields of development;

(d) To submit reports, information and recommendations concerning the enhancement of the role of women in development.

Institutional arrangements for policy formulation, implementation, monitoring, review and appraisal of initiatives to incorporate women in development have been established to enable the State Minister to function effectively. As a member of the Cabinet, the State Minister interacts with other ministers and members of the Cabinet through Cabinet meetings. In addition, monthly consultative meetings are held with government agencies under the coordination of the Coordinating Minister for People's Welfare, and close cooperation is maintained with the National Development Planning Board (BAPENAS) and other technical departments.

While the Office of the State Minister for the Role of Women is responsible for policy formulation, planning, coordination and advocacy, the implementation of women in development programmes remains the responsibility of various sectoral ministries and departments. Almost all departments are involved in the implementation of programmes to enhance the role of women in development. Programme officers are located within the hierarchical structure of the ministries, and the activities of various ministries/departments are coordinated through working groups established in the Office of the State Minister for the Role of Women. At the subnational levels, the programmes or projects are carried out by field offices of the sectoral ministries in cooperation with the subnational governmental machineries.

As a result of the various measures adopted, there has been considerable improvement in the status and role of Indonesian women over the years. They have achieved important gains in access to education, health care and economic opportunities. Nevertheless, there are significant gaps in achievement between males and females in various areas. For example, although girls and boys are now being enrolled in equal proportions at the primary level, female participation at secondary and higher levels of education continues to be considerably lower than that of males. While female labour-force participation rates have increased, a large proportion of female labour is in the informal sector and female earnings are substantially lower than those of males. Women's participation in the formal political process is very low; they are grossly under-represented in the legislative bodies at the national and local levels.

It is thus clear that additional measures ought to be taken to further enhance the participation of women in education, health, employment and politics and in other fields. The formulation of appropriate measures and programmes would, of course, call for the collection and analysis of relevant data and information highlighting the issues and concerns as well as pinpointing the geographic areas and regions and groups of population that need priority attention. Fortunately, Indonesia has a relatively well developed mechanism for the systematic collection and analysis of a wide variety of data relevant to women's concerns. While most of these data have been disaggregated by gender, there is still a need to initiate action for the collection and analysis of additional data. The present profile on women attempts to highlight the gaps in data and information and also provides a framework for continued analysis of data so as to give a more comprehensive picture of the situation of women vis-à-vis men.

A. HIGHLIGHTS

The setting

1. Indonesia, the world's largest archipelago, consists of five main islands and 30 small archipelagos comprising nearly 17,000 islands and islets, not all of which are inhabited. The total land area of the country is 1.9 million square kilometres.

2. After nearly 135 years of foreign rule, Indonesian national leaders declared independence in August 1945. Today, the Republic of Indonesia is a unitary State in which the executive power is vested in the President. For administrative purposes, the country is divided into 27 provinces, which are further subdivided into regencies and municipalities.

3. Indonesia is the world's fourth most populous country, with an estimated population of 197.5 million in 1995. The average annual growth rate of the population declined from 2.3 per cent in the 1960s to about 1.5 per cent during the period 1990-1995.

4. The regional distribution of the population is very uneven, with about 62 per cent of the nation's population being concentrated in the islands of Java and Bali, which account for only 7.0 per cent of the total land area. A government-sponsored transmigration programme has resettled a substantial number of people from the most densely populated islands to other sparsely populated areas of the country.

5. Despite the common ethnic base of the vast majority of the population, the country is characterized by a high degree of linguistic, religious, cultural and social diversity. About 87 per cent of the people are Moslems, and Indonesia has the world's largest Islamic population.

6. From a situation of extreme difficulties inherited by Indonesia's New Order Government in 1966, the Indonesian economy emerged in remarkably transformed and resilient form at the close of the country's 25-year period of planned development in 1993/94. Since the early 1970s, gross domestic product (GDP) growth has averaged almost 7 per cent per annum and per capita income was estimated at US$ 1,000 in 1995. The proportion of the population living in poverty has been drastically reduced, from 43 per cent in the mid-1970s to 14 per cent in 1993.

7. The continued commitment of the government to human resources development has resulted in Indonesia launching one of the world's most successful expansions of school systems. The country has almost achieved universal primary education, and over the years there has been a steady increase in the level of educational attainment and literacy rates of the people.

8. The emphasis placed on the provision of basic health care has resulted in rapid expansion of the health infrastructure throughout the county. This in turn has resulted in a consider-able lowering of morbidity and mortality. The general death rate, as well as infant mortality rates, have been drastically cut over the past three decades, resulting in a rise in life expectancy at birth from 37.5 in the early 1960s to 62.5 during the period 1990-1995.

Women's profile

1. Indonesia is one of the few countries in the Asian and Pacific region in which females have outnumbered males in the total population at various census counts since 1961. In 1990, there were 100.6 females per 100 males in the country.

2. Accelerated declines in fertility and mortality rates have resulted in significant changes in the age structure of the population; the percentage share of children under 15 years of age has been constantly decreasing, with concomitant increases in the proportion of persons in the working ages 15-64 years. An important consequence of these shifts has been the steady increase in the number as well as relative share of women in reproductive ages 15-44 years.

3. In recent years, the proportion of persons aged 15 years and over reported as never married has been increasing for both males and females, although this proportion is significantly lower among females than males. The proportion of the population living in a state of marital disruption (widowed or divorced) is considerably higher among females than males.

4. The expansion in the education system that had taken place during the past three decades has benefited females more than males. At the primary level, more girls than boys are enrolled; however, at higher levels of education, female participation rates are significantly lower than male rates.

5. The level of educational attainment of both males and females has increased over the years. The proportion of women aged 10 years and over with no schooling or incomplete schooling has been declining. Female literacy rates have been increasing faster than male rates, thereby narrowing the gender gap in these rates. Nevertheless, in 1990 nearly 68 per cent of the 215 million illiterate Indonesians were women.

6. In recent decades, the government has been implementing several health programmes aimed at improving the health of children and women, and an increasing number of women have been involved in these programmes as both beneficiaries and front-line health workers.

7. The most common diseases among both males and females are infections of the respiratory organs, infections of the skin, diarrhoea, malaria, nutritional disorders, and eye diseases. The relative share of morbidity among children under five years is greatly out of proportion to their share in the total population. On an average, each child under five years of age contracts four diseases a year.

8. Considerable progress has been made in reducing infant and child mortality rates; however, their current levels are still relatively high compared with a number of other countries in the region. Mortality rates among females infants are significantly lower than among male infants in both urban and rural areas.

9. Despite the decline over the years, the maternal mortality rate is also still high in Indonesia. An important factor contributing to the high rate is the very low proportion of deliveries assisted by trained health personnel.

10. The reduction in mortality rates has resulted in an increase in life expectancy at birth, from 54.0 years in 1980 to 64.9 years in 1994 for females, and from 50.9 to 61.2 years for males. Thus, an Indonesian woman today can expect to live, on an average, 3.7 years longer than her male counterpart.

Women in family life

1. Although a large number of Indonesian families are of the extended type, there is an increasing tendency towards nuclearization of families throughout the country, as evidenced by the rise in the percentage share of families with less than five members.

2. As in most developing countries, women continue to shoulder the major share of household chores, often working longer hours than men. Nevertheless, they play an important role in the decisions relating to family matters.

3. The number of female-headed households has been increasing in recent years. The majority of female household heads are over 50 years of age and mostly widowed. Women usually become heads of households only upon the death of their husbands.

4. Socio-cultural norms and values have traditionally favoured universal and early marriage. However, recent decades have witnessed an increasing tendency among young persons to refrain from early marriage and enter into wedlock at a later stage, resulting in a rise in the average age at first marriage.

5. The nature of the marriage institution itself is undergoing significant transformation, from a traditional pattern of arranged marriages to a modern one characterized by self-selection of partners.

6. Together with shifts in marriage patterns, there are also significant changes in the reproductive behaviour of married couples, as exemplified by the increasing desire for smaller families and sharp reductions in the number of children born to ever-married women. The total fertility rate declined from 5.6 in 1971 to 2.8 in 1994.

7. Data from successive surveys conclusively point to a continuing increase in the knowledge about and use of contraceptives among married women, with the vast majority using modern methods. Contraceptive use is higher among urban than among rural women, and among the more educated than among those with no education.

8. Marital disruption appears to be a more serious problem among women than men. A higher proportion among females than males are either widowed or divorced. Available evidence suggests that early marriages result in early family dissolution.

9. Accurate data on domestic violence against women are not available. However, it is generally accepted that wife abuse/battery is a fairly common phenomenon. Women also constitute the majority of victims in reported cases of violence in the country.

Women in economic life

1. Traditionally, Indonesian women had played an important role in the country's economic development efforts. Women's economic activities, especially those belonging to the poorer segments of the population, have by and large been closely associated with their responsibilities in the family.

2. Labour-force participation rates for Indonesian women have been increasing rapidly in recent decades, and this increase is especially large among young adult women. Despite these increases, the female labour-force participation rate is still considerably lower than the male rate and is among the lowest in the region.

3. During the 1980s, there were significant shifts in the sectoral composition of employment for both males and females. Although agriculture still accounts for nearly half the female labour force, about 8.4 million women were employed in the service sector and another 3.6 million in the manufacturing industries. Within the service sector, a large increase in women workers has taken place in the trade sector.

4. A larger proportion among female than male workers is concentrated in low-paying, part-time and lower status jobs, an important reason for this differential being the relatively low level of education and skill training of women.

5. Since 1980, a striking increase has been evident in women's participation in the formal sector. Yet, in 1990 approximately 61 per cent of the male and 69 per cent of the female workforce were in the informal sector. Within the informal sector, a considerably higher proportion among female compared with male workers were engaged as unpaid family workers. Between 1980 and 1990, the number of female unpaid family workers increased by about 4.1 million, the corresponding increase being only 1.1 million in the case of males.

6. In general, the average number of hours worked are lower for female than for male workers, and the numbers of hours worked by women considerably shorter than those for men in the agriculture, mining and transport sectors.

7. The average earnings of women are also considerably lower than those of men for each level of educational attainment. However, the average earnings of a female worker with tertiary level of education are nearly five times those of a female worker with no formal education.

8. Female unemployment rates are also higher than the rates for males. Unemployment rates for both males and females vary considerably by age, being higher at younger than older ages. In 1990, the unemployment rate among urban females (7.4 per cent) was nearly three times the rate of 2.7 per cent reported for rural females.

9. There are several programmes operated by governmental and non-governmental organizations to provide credit facilities for women to set up their own income-earning activities.

Women in public life

1. Although an increasing proportion of eligible women have been voting at various elections, women's representation in key political decision-making bodies has changed very little over the years. In 1993, women constituted only about 12 per cent of total parliamentarians and 8 per cent of the membership of the People's Consultative Assembly.

2. The overall representation of women in the legislative bodies at the provincial level is also small, with their relative share remaining constant in 11 provinces, decreasing in 6 and increasing in 10 provinces between 1987 and 1992.

3. Women's participation in decision-making at the highest executive and judicial levels is also relatively limited; only 12 per cent of the members of the Supreme Court, 5 per cent of the Supreme Advisory Council, and 2 per cent of the members of the State Audit Board are women.

4. Although women are being recruited into the civil service in much larger numbers than previously, the placement of women in key managerial and decision-making roles is occurring at a much slower pace.

5. Women are very much under-represented in the foreign or diplomatic service; in 1994, only 4 of the 76 ambassadors and one of the 17 consuls-general were women.

6. An increasing number of Indonesian women engage in development activities at the village or community levels.

B. THE SETTING

1. Geography

The Republic of Indonesia, the world's largest archipelago, extends more than 4,800 kilometres from east to west and 2,000 kilometres from north to south between the southern tip of the Asian mainland and Australia. Physically, the archipelago consists of five major islands, Sumatera, Java, Kalimantan, Sulawesi, and Irian Jaya, and about 30 small archipelagos comprising nearly 17,000 islands and islets, not all of which are inhabited or inhabitable. More than 80 per cent of the Indonesian territory is covered with water, and the total land area is 1.9 million square kilometres. The five main islands together constitute about 92 per cent of the total land area.

In terms of geography, the country lies on one eighth of the earth's circumference and stretches through three time zones. It has two distinct ecological zones having different types of flora and fauna, and characterized by variations due to differences in topography, including snow-capped mountains in Irian Jaya, the dry savannah of Nusa Tenggara, or humid areas in other parts of this equatorial country. Indonesia's climate is tropical, with two seasons; the dry season extends from May to October, and the rainy season from November to April.

2. History

In the past, the territories now comprising Indonesia had never constituted a single political entity. A number of important empires and kingdoms had existed, each endowed with more or less comparable resources to protect their separate identities. Prior to the sixteenth century, these kingdoms had established close commercial and cultural relations with India, and consequently the administration of these kingdoms as well as the culture of the people came to be strongly influenced by Hindu and Buddhist beliefs and practices.

The quest for spices in the fifteenth and sixteenth centuries resulted in Europeans, initially Spaniards and Portuguese and subsequently British and Dutch, being interested in Indonesia. Apart from the establishment of a Portuguese colonial outpost in the eastern half of the island of Timor, the Spaniards and Portuguese contributed very little to the subsequent colonial history of Indonesia. After a brief period of British occupation (1811-1816), the Dutch gradually but effectively began to establish their control over various parts of the country, and Indonesia came to be known as the Dutch East Indies. Dutch rule ended in 1942 when the Japanese occupied the country. Within three days after the surrender of the Japanese to the Allies, the Indonesian national leaders declared independence, on 17 August 1945.

Since proclaiming its independence, Indonesia has experienced several political shifts. In 1948, a rebellion by the Communist Party took place in Madiun. Up until the end of 1949, when the Dutch gave up control over Indonesia, there were disputes against the ruling democratic republic. Some factions, supported by the Dutch, formed the Federation of Indonesian Republics, which lasted less than one year. From 1950 to 1959, Indonesia faced several political problems, including the adoption of a multi-party system, which resulted in political and economic instability, and rebellions caused by ideological, ethnic and racial differences. The history of the Republic of Indonesia had a turning point after an aborted coup by the Communist Party in September 1965. In 1966, President Suharto began a new era with the establishment of the New Order Government, which is oriented towards overall development.

3. Political and administrative systems

In 1950, the Republic of Indonesia became a unitary State in which the executive power is vested in the President, who is elected to a five-year term by the People's Consultative

Assembly, which meets to decide general policy and elect the President. Half of its 1,000 members are appointees representing regional assemblies, political parties and other groups. The House of Representatives contributes the other 500 members of the Assembly, with 100 members of the armed services and other appointees, and 400 directly elected by citizens who are married or are over 17 years of age. The Cabinet is appointed by and is responsible to the President.

For convenience of administration, Indonesia is divided into 27 provinces, each province consisting of regencies and municipalities. At present there are 243 regencies and 60 municipalities in all. The next lower administrative unit is the subdistrict, then the village. In 1993, there were 3,879 subdistricts, 7,585 urban villages, and 58,097 rural villages.

4. Population size and distribution

The population of Indonesia, according to the last census held in October 1990, was 179.4 million, 32.5 million more than the 146.9 million enumerated at the previous census held in October 1980. Recent estimates prepared by the United Nations, however, indicate a population of 182.8 million in 1990 and 197.5 million in 1995. Indonesia is currently the fourth most populous country in the world, next to China, India and the United States of America, and the most populous in South-East Asia.

Since the mid-1960s, Indonesia has been experiencing a high rate of population growth averaging more than 2.3 per cent per annum, owing to a significant decline in mortality resulting from improved nutrition and medical care. The growth rate decelerated to less than 2.0 per cent per annum between 1980 and 1990 owing to a reduction in fertility. The national average growth rate, however, conceals the marked variation in this rate among the major islands. During the period 1980-1990, the annual rate of population growth ranged from a low of 1.64 per cent in Java to 2.5 per cent in Bali and Nusa Tenggara to 3.0 per cent in Kalimantan and to a high of 3.3 per cent in Maluku and Irian Jaya. According to recent United Nations estimates, Indonesia's population growth rate averaged 1.54 per cent during the period 1990-1995.

Another important demographic feature is the uneven distribution of the population across the various islands. For instance, in 1993 about 60 per cent of the country's population was concentrated in Java, which only constituted about 7 per cent of the total land area. Consequently, Java's population density of 848.5 per cent per square kilometre was among the highest in the world. On the other hand, in the outer island of Irian Jaya, with about 22 per cent of the land area and less than one per cent of the population, the density was a mere 4.3 persons per square kilometre (table 1 and annex table B.1).

Table 1. Area, population and population density by major island group: 1993

Island group	Land area		Estimated population (1993)		Density (per square kilometre)
	Square kilometres	Percent-age	Number	Percent-age	
Java and Madura	132 186	6.9	112 158 200	59.6	848.5
Sumatera	473 481	24.9	39 232 800	20.8	82.9
Kalimantan	539 460	28.3	9 959 800	5.3	18.5
Sulawesi	189 216	9.9	13 279 000	7.1	70.2
Bali	5 561	0.3	2 856 000	1.5	513.6
Nusa Tenggara	68 053	3.6	7 011 600	3.7	103.0
Maluku	74 505	3.9	2 001 200	1.1	26.9
Irian Jaya	421 981	22.2	1 828 700	1.0	4.3
Indonesia	1 904 443	100.0	188 327 300	100.0	98.9

Source: Central Bureau of Statistics.

In order to reduce the imbalance in the distribution of population, the government initiated a programme of voluntary resettlement known as "transmigration". This programme enables people to move from the densely populated islands of Java, Bali and Madura to more sparsely populated and less developed areas, including Sulawesi, Kalimantan and Irian Jaya. Government encouragement and assistance for households to move come in the form of the provision of two hectares of land per family, housing, certain farming and household equipment and basic foodstuffs for up to two years. The government also provides for the establishment of basic community infrastructure, such as schools and health centres. Nearly 2 million people are estimated to have taken part in the transmigration programme up to 1995.

A combination of surplus labour in rural areas and growing industrial and service sectors in the urban areas has led to increasing urbanization. The proportion of the population living in areas classified as urban increased from 22.4 per cent in 1980 to 30.9 per cent in 1990, with the average rate of population growth amounting to 5.4 per cent in urban areas compared with 0.8 per cent in rural areas. The highest level of urbanization was recorded for Java, where more than 35 per cent of the population reside in urban areas, and which has four of the five largest cities in Indonesia.

5. Ethnicity and religion

Although precise data are not available in regard to the ethnic composition of the population, there is a considerable degree of ethnic homogeneity. With the exception of small remnants of aboriginal people, the indigenous population of most of the major islands is largely of Malay stock, while the remaining small proportion is of Melanesian stock. The largest non-indigenous group is Chinese, most of whom have lived in Indonesia for generations. They are mainly descendants of immigrants who originally came from the then Fukien and Kwangtung provinces of China. Over 80 per cent of the Chinese reside in the towns and cities of Java and Sumatera, where they are mostly engaged in trade.

Although the people of Indonesia have, by and large, a common ethnic base, there is marked linguistic, cultural and religious diversity in the country. There are about 250 separate regional languages and dialects, most of which have an Austronesian (Malayo-Polynesian) base. The major exceptions are those of West Irian, where Papuan languages are used; and some of the Moluccas where the North Halmaheran language family is found. In the most populous Java-Madura-Bali inner-island complex, 4 major languages are spoken, while there are 15 on Sumatera. The national language is Bahasa Indonesia, evolved from a Malay dialect spoken in East Sumatera.

According to the 1990 census, 87.2 per cent of the Indonesians are Moslems; and Indonesia has the world's largest Islamic population. In some Indonesian provinces, adherents of other religious faiths are in the majority: Hindus in Bali (90.3 per cent); Catholics in East Nusa Tenggara (52.9 per cent) and in East Timor (90.7 per cent); and Protestants in Irian Jaya (60.0 per cent).

Despite the diversity in language, religion and culture, the Indonesian way of life is based on *Pancasila* (the Five Basic Principles) as the state philosophy. These principles are: belief in one supreme god; justice and civility among people; the unity of Indonesia; democracy through deliberation and consensus among representatives; and social justice for all.

6. The economy

Although Indonesia has been one of the most richly endowed countries in terms of natural resources, and also had the capacity to produce a wide range of agricultural commodities, the first two decades of Indonesia's post-independence economic history were characterized by dislocation and decline. Domestic political upheavals and economic mismanagement, together with weak international commodity markets, prevented the effective rehabilitation of an economy which had already been seriously disrupted by three years of Japanese wartime occupation and a four-year armed struggle for independence. Consequently, Indonesia was one of the poorest countries in the world, with a per capita gross national product estimated at only US$ 50.

However, since 1969, Indonesian development policies and objectives were clearly spelt out in a series of five-year development plans, known by the acronym REPELITA, and in the Broad Guidelines of State Policies (GBHN). The first four plans placed greater emphasis on the development of the agriculture sector, but thereafter the emphasis shifted to the manufacturing and service sectors. The focus of the current five-year plan is on manufacturing industries, especially those that are export-oriented.

Since the early 1970s, GDP growth has averaged almost 7 per cent per annum, placing Indonesia among the 10 top developing countries in terms of overall growth. Economic growth has also been broadbased, providing jobs in agriculture, services and manufacturing, and expanding social services in health and education. In the 1980s, Indonesia faced a series of severe external shocks including the collapse of oil prices, the rise in international rates, and the depreciation of the United States dollar. The average growth rate fell to 3.3 per cent in 1983 but improved slightly to 3.6 per cent in 1987. The government responded to the crisis by deregulation of the economy and implementing policies to boost non-oil exports. Structural adjustment measures were also undertaken, including devaluation and a more actively managed exchange rate, and strong fiscal policy measures to mobilize resources and restrain public expenditure.

As a result of the pragmatic policies and measures, the economy recovered and the growth rate increased to 7.0 per cent in 1990 and to 8.2 per cent in 1995. The major driving force behind this recovery was the private sector, which contributed over 70 per cent of the total GDP growth during the period 1983-1991. The strong growth in the non-oil economy created productive new job opportunities that reduced unemployment, raised real wages, increased real incomes and consumption, and contributed to a reduction in poverty. The proportion of the Indonesian population living below the poverty line declined from 43 per cent in the mid-1970s to 29 per cent in 1980 and further to about 14

per cent in 1993. In 1995, per capita income was estimated at US$ 1,000, and GDP per head at US$ 1,023.

In terms of economic structure, agriculture has traditionally been the predominant sector, until it was superseded by the manufacturing sector, in 1991. The agricultural sector comprises five subsectors: food crops, cash crops, animal husbandry, fishing, and forestry. Of these, the food-crop subsector is the most important in terms of income and employment generation. In 1994, the agricultural sector accounted for about 17 per cent of GNP and employed 48 per cent of the labour force. The manufacturing sector contributed 23.4 per cent of GNP and employed 15 per cent of the workforce in 1994 (table 2; see also figure 1). The development of tourism is being strongly encouraged through the construction of small and medium-sized hotels, and a tourist complex at Nusa Dua on South Bali.

7. Social infrastructure

(a) Education system

The current education system in Indonesia consists of formal education and non-formal education (figure 2). The formal education system consists of three major levels: primary

Table 2. Gross domestic product, 1994, at 1993 constant prices by sector

(Billions of rupiahs)

Sector	Value	Percentage
Agriculture, livestock, forestry and fishery	59 287.4	16.7
Mining and quarrying	33 261.7	9.4
Manufacturing industries	82 725.7	23.4
Electricity, gas and water supply	3 707.4	1.0
Construction	25 857.5	7.3
Trade, hotel and restaurant	59 350.5	16.7
Transport and communication	25 065.8	7.1
Banking and other financial intermediares	30 901.0	8.7
Services	34 285.1	9.7
Total	354 442.0	100.0

Source: Central Bureau of Statistics.

Figure 1. Rate of growth of four major sectors of gross domestic product

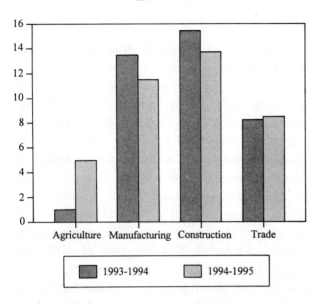

Source: **Central Bureau of Statistics,** *The 1996 Economic Condition and the 1997 Prediction.*

education, secondary education and higher or tertiary education.

Primary education consists of pre-school (a one- to three-year programme), and elementary school (a six-year programme for children at ages 6-7 years). The elementary school programme is designed to provide basic education to all children between ages 7 and 12 years. Secondary education consists of junior secondary and senior secondary school and is of two types: general education, which aims to prepare students with the required knowledge to continue to the higher education stream; and vocational education, designed to equip students with adequate skills to enter the labour market or to continue with higher professional education. The junior secondary school programme provides education to children at ages 13-15 years, while the senior secondary schools enrol students aged 16-18 years. Higher education consists of degree and non-degree programmes and is provided through universities, teacher training institutes and other higher educational institutions.

In order to expand educational opportunities for those who have missed formal education, a number of complementary or alternative programmes of non-formal education have been devised. These include Program Kajor, designed to give the out-of-school population a chance to attain the basic knowledge, attitude and skills relevant to development, as well as adult programmes of literacy and other adult education programmes.

Figure 2. Education system in Indonesia

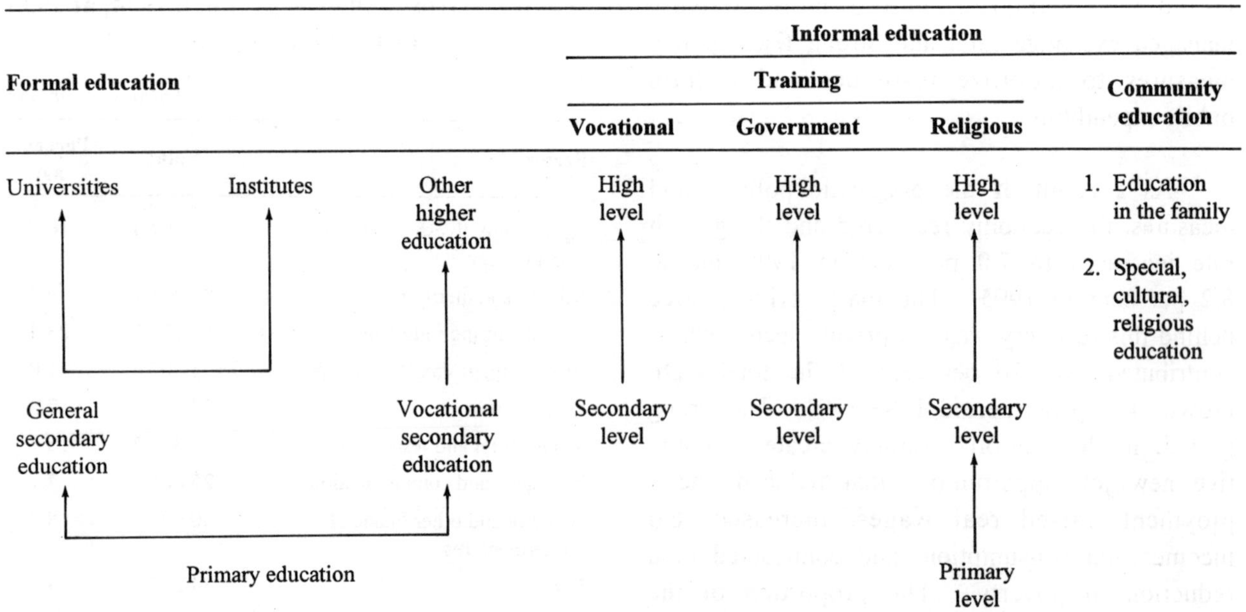

Formal education			Informal education			Community education
			Training			
			Vocational	Government	Religious	
Universities	Institutes	Other higher education	High level	High level	High level	1. Education in the family
						2. Special, cultural, religious education
General secondary education		Vocational secondary education	Secondary level	Secondary level	Secondary level	
Primary education					Primary level	

Source: Economic and Social Commission for Asia and the Pacific, *Human Resources Development: Effectiveness of Programme Delivery at the Local Level in Countries of the ESCAP Region,* Development Papers No. 16 (Bangkok, 1994).

Since independence, the government has placed great emphasis on human resources development, and sustained social improvements are an outstanding achievement characterizing the country's development during the last three decades. The high priority given to education has seen Indonesia launching one of the world's most successful expansions of school systems along with improving the quality of education. The government's commitment to the development of education is reflected in the adoption of universal primary education as a major policy objective, and in the efforts made to democratize education so as to give all children equal opportunities for education and improve the quality of education imparted.

In 1974, the INPRES (Presidential Instruction) programme for primary schools and facilities was initiated, through which tens of thousands of new school buildings were constructed during the second, third and fourth five-year plans throughout the country. At the same time, expenditure on the recruitment and training of teachers was dramatically expanded. Primary school fees were abolished in 1977/78 in an effort to further improve access and equity. A policy of compulsory primary education was introduced in 1984, and 10 years later Indonesia introduced nine years of compulsory basic education to encourage extended participation in formal education among the 6-15 year-old age group. Considerable progress has also been achieved in regard to the expansion of secondary and tertiary educational facilities, and large numbers of schools and universities have been established and equipped by both the public and private sectors since the mid-1960s.

As a result of the various policies and programmes adopted since independence, Indonesia has achieved substantial progress in education. The number of pupils at various levels of education had increased tremendously over the years and available data indicate that the participation rate at the primary level increased from 41.4 per cent of the relevant age population in 1968 to 95.0 per cent in 1995/96. Indonesia is now within striking distance of achieving universal primary education. The participation rate at the secondary level almost trebled, from 13.1 to 38.6 per cent, while at the tertiary level the increase was from 1.6 to 10.0 per cent, between 1968 and 1994/95 (table 3). The overall illiteracy rate in Indonesia is fairly low, having declined from 39 per cent of the total population in 1971 to 23 per cent in 1990.

(b) Health services

Throughout the 1960s and during the early years of the first five-year plan (REPELITA 1969-1974), relatively low priority was given to health and nutrition. However, during the second plan period (REPELITA II 1974-1979), high priority was accorded to the development of health services, particularly improving access to these services in the rural areas. Since then, Indonesia has made considerable progress in building up a health-care delivery system comprising a network of primary, secondary and tertiary facilities. In 1994/95, there were 835

Table 3. Student enrolment and participation rates by level of education: 1968 and 1995/96

Level of education	1968		1995/96	
	Number of pupils (thousands)	Participation rate (percentage)[a]	Number of pupils (thousands)	Participation rate (percentage)[a]
Primary education	7 403	41.4	24 295.0	95.0
Secondary education[b]	1 632	13.1	10 534.0	40.5
Tertiary education[c]	156	1.6	3 167.9	12.8

Source: National Development Information Office, *Indonesia Source Book, 1996.*

[a] Percentage of children in relevant age groups attending educational establishments.
[b] Junior and senior high schools.
[c] Excluding religious seminaries.

13

general hospitals and 906 specialized hospitals with a total number of 128,708 beds located in provincial and district capitals. But the main source of modern public health service for the vast majority of Indonesians residing in rural areas is the primary-level system of community health centres, subcentres and mobile health centres, which increased tremendously in number between 1968 and 1994/95 (table 4).

Table 4. Public health facilities, services and personnel: 1968 and 1994/95

Facilities/services/personnel	Number	
	1968	1994/95
Public health centres	1 227	6 984
Auxiliary public health centres	..	20 477
Mobile public health centres	..	6 552
General hospitals	798	835
Beds in general hospitals	63 737	98 952
Specialized hospitals	327	906
Beds in specialized hospitals	21 738	29 756
Doctors	5 000	25 135[a]
Nurses and midwives	7 630	118 555[a]
Paramedics and health workers	1 182	187 501[a]

Source: National Development Information Office, *Indonesia Source Book,* 1996.

[a] Data for the year 1992.

Two dots (. .) indicate that data are not available.

The community health centre (*puskasmas*) is the cornerstone of the country's public health system, providing basic medical care, MCH services, family planning services, communicable disease control (including immunizations), hygiene and sanitation, nutrition, community health education, school health and dental treatment. A fully staffed centre is headed by a doctor, assisted by several trained paramedical staff such as nurses and auxiliary health workers. Today, there are about 7,000 centres, each serving an average of over 32,000 persons. The sub-health centres, numbering a little over 20,000, are located in the main villages and provide basic MCH care, including vaccination and health education, serving on average a population ranging from 3,000 to 10,000.

Over the years, Indonesia has made significant strides towards reducing the incidence of morbidity and mortality and improving the health status of its people. Major health problems of a few decades ago, such as malaria, intestinal parasites and endemic diseases (e.g. dysentery, typhoid, typhus and cholera) have today been more or less brought under control. There has been a substantial increase in the proportion of the population provided with access to safe drinking water in both urban and rural areas. Consequently, the crude death rate is estimated to have declined from 26.1 per 1,000 population in 1960-1965 to 8.4 in 1990-1995, and the infant mortality rate from 160 per 1,000 live births to 58 per 1,000 live births during the same period. Life expectancy at birth is estimated to have increased from 37.5 years in 1960-1965 to 62.7 years in 1990-1995.

In recent years, efforts to advance health facilities have been carried out in partnership with private sector health care investment and management. Investments by the private sector, including foreign investors, have resulted in the establishment of modern hospital facilities equipped with the latest medical knowledge.

C. WOMEN'S PROFILE

1. Demographic characteristics

(a) Gender balance

Data from the censuses and surveys indicate that in Indonesia females have consistently outnumbered males in the total population, although this numerical gap between the two sexes has been gradually narrowing over the years, as is reflected in the trend of various indicators. Between 1961 and 1990, there was a decline in the proportionate share of females in the total population from 50.7 to 50.1 per cent, and in the number of females per 100 males from 102.8 to 100.6. Consequently, there has been an increase in the sex ratio, or number of males per 100 females, from 97.3 in 1961 to 99.4 in 1990 (table 5).

The reported excess of females in the total population is a demographic feature of only a very few countries in the region. In Indonesia, this phenomenon has been the result of a combination of factors. Although reliable data are

Table 5. Enumerated population classified by sex, percentage female, and females/100 males and males/100 females: censuses of 1961 to 1990 and 1985 Population Survey

Year	Population (thousands)			Percent-age female	Females/ 100 males	Males/ 100 females
	Both sexes	Male	Female			
1961	96 318.8	47 493.9	48 824.9	50.69	102.80	97.27
1971	118 907.5	58 878.3	60 029.2	50.48	101.95	98.08
1980	146 776.5	72 951.7	73 824.8	50.30	101.20	98.82
1985	164 047.0	81 644.1	82 402.9	50.23	100.93	99.08
1990	179 247.8	89 375.7	89 872.1	50.14	100.56	99.45

Source: Central Bureau of Statistics.

not available, it is generally believed that a substantially higher number of males than females died during the three-year Japanese occupation occupation (1942-1945) and during the more than four years of fighting with the Netherlands to secure independence. Further, estimates indicate that over the past four decades mortality rates have been higher among males than among females, and consequently life expectancy at birth has been increasingly higher for females than for males.

The sex ratio varies by age group and residence. The numerical distribution of the population enumerated at the 1980 and 1990 censuses by age group and sex is given in annex table C.1, and the indicators of gender balance by age group are shown in table 6. It will be noted from table 6 that in 1990 males exceeded females at younger age groups 0-19 years owing to the male-favoured sex ratio at birth and better survival chances for males at these ages. From age 20 years

Table 6. Indicators of gender balance by age group: censuses of 1980 and 1990

Age group	1980 census			1990 census		
	Percent-age female	Females/ 100 males	Males/ 100 females	Percent-age female	Females/ 100 males	Males/ 100 females
0-4	48.9	95.6	104.6	48.7	95.0	105.2
5-9	49.0	96.2	103.9	48.6	94.7	105.6
10-14	48.1	92.7	107.9	48.6	94.5	105.8
15-19	50.7	103.0	97.1	49.7	98.8	101.2
20-24	54.0	117.3	85.2	53.0	112.7	88.7
25-29	50.4	101.4	98.5	52.3	109.5	91.3
30-34	51.0	104.1	96.1	50.3	101.2	98.8
35-39	51.2	105.0	95.2	48.2	93.2	107.3
40-44	50.4	101.8	98.2	50.4	101.5	98.4
45-49	51.1	104.4	95.7	50.8	103.2	96.9
50-54	50.2	101.0	99.0	50.8	103.3	96.8
55-59	49.4	97.5	102.5	52.0	108.1	92.4
60-64	52.2	109.1	91.7	51.0	104.0	96.2
65-69	52.0	108.4	92.3	51.7	106.9	93.6
70-74	55.8	126.2	79.2	53.7	114.5	87.3
75+	54.5	119.9	83.4	56.0	127.3	78.5
Not stated	43.3	76.4	130.8	50.0	100.2	99.9
All ages	50.3	101.2	98.8	50.1	100.6	99.4

Source: Central Bureau of Statistics.

onwards, females outnumber males at all five-year age groups except the age group 35-39 years, and the preponderance of females is more marked at the very old ages 70 years and over, reflecting the longer life expectancy for females.

Data from the 1980 and 1990 censuses as well as the 1985 Intercensal Population Survey show that the pattern of gender balance varies between urban and rural areas of the country. At the 1980 census there was a slight excess of males over females in the urban areas, while females significantly outnumbered males in the rural areas. However, according to the 1990 census data, the number of females was higher than the number of males in both the urban and rural areas, but the number of males per 100 females was slightly higher in urban compared with rural areas (table 7). The slightly higher sex ratio in urban compared with rural areas is largely due to the fact that rural males tend to migrate towards urban areas to avail themselves of the better employment opportunities in those areas.

It will also be noted from annex table C.2 that the sex ratio varies from a low of 95.5 in South Sulawesi and 95.9 in West Sumatera to a high of 110.5 in Irian Jaya and 110.9 in East Kalimantan. The very low sex ratio observed for West Sumatera is largely due to the *merantau* norms which require men to emigrate temporarily and to return to their native village with wealth. In 1990, there was a deficit of males (or excess of females) in 11 provinces. The numerical balance between the sexes in various provinces is by and large determined by mortality and migration patterns in each of the provinces.

(b) Age structure

The percentage distribution of the population by conventional five-year age groups and by gender and residence for the census years 1980 and 1990 is shown in annex table C.3. It is clear from the table that there was a general decline in the age-specific proportions with advancing age for both males and females in 1980 as well as in 1990. However, as a result of the fairly rapid decline in fertility and mortality, there have been significant changes in the age structure of the population during the past two decades (figure 3). It is evident from annex table C.3 and figure 3 that between 1980 and 1990, while the proportions at younger ages have been declining, there has been an increase in the proportions of those in older age groups for both males and females in urban as well as in rural areas.

Table 7. Distribution of the enumerated population by residence and sex, and indicators of sex balance: 1980, 1985 and 1990

Census/survey year and residence	Enumerated/estimated population			Sex-balance indicators		
	Both sexes	Male	Female	Percentage female	Males/100 females	Females/100 males
1980 census						
Indonesia	146 776 473	72 951 670	73 824 803	50.3	98.8	101.2
Urban	32 845 769	16 441 891	16 403 878	49.9	100.2	99.8
Rural	113 930 704	56 509 779	57 420 925	50.4	98.4	101.6
1985 survey						
Indonesia	164 046 988	81 644 112	82 402 876	50.2	99.1	100.9
Urban	43 029 526	21 435 629	21 593 897	50.2	99.3	100.7
Rural	121 017 462	60 208 483	60 808 979	50.2	99.0	101.0
1990 census						
Indonesia	179 247 783	89 375 677	89 872 106	50.1	99.4	100.6
Urban	55 433 790	27 683 319	27 750 471	50.1	99.8	100.2
Rural	123 813 993	61 692 358	62 121 635	50.2	99.3	100.7

Sources: Central Bureau of Statistics, *Population of Indonesia: Results of the Sub-sample of the 1980 Population Census; Results of the 1985 Intercensal Population Survey;* and *Results of the 1990 Population Census.*

Figure 3. Age structure of the population: 1971, 1980, 1990 and 2000

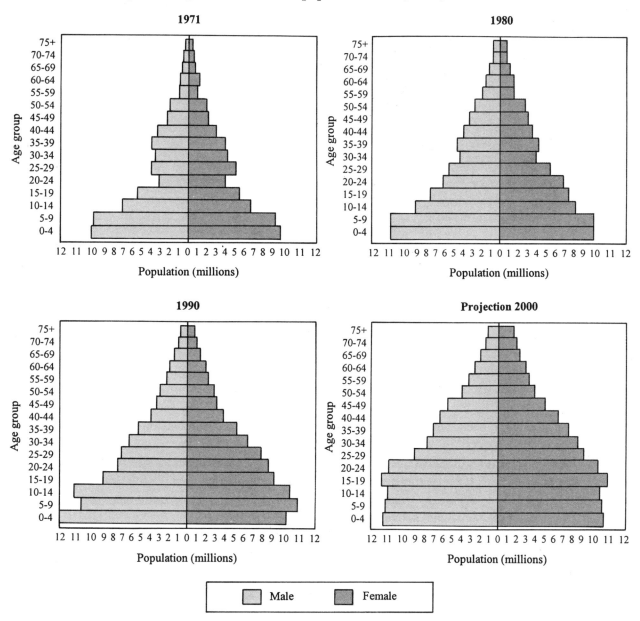

Source: Central Bureau of Statistics.

A clearer picture of the changes in the age composition of the population between 1971 and 1990 is obtained by examining the proportionate distribution of the population according to three broad age groups: 0-14 years (child population), 15-64 years (working age population), and 65 years and over (elderly population), shown in table 8.

It will be noted from table 8 that the proportion of all children under 15 years of age has been constantly decreasing, from 44.0 per cent in 1971 to 36.6 per cent in 1990, and that

this decline had occurred among both boys and girls. It will also be noted that in all three years for which data are presented, the proportion aged 0-14 years has been higher among males than among females, and in 1990, children constituted 37.7 per cent among all males and 35.6 per cent among all females. The relative share of persons in productive or working ages 15-64 years, which has always been higher for females than for males, increased between 1971 and 1990, when 58.7 per cent of all males as compared with 60.4 per cent of all females belonged to the productive age group.

Table 8. Percentage distribution of the population according to broad age groups and dependency ratios: 1971, 1980 and 1990

Age group	1971			1980			1990		
	Both sexes	Male	Female	Both sexes	Male	Female	Both sexes	Male	Female
0-14	44.0	45.0	42.6	40.9	42.3	39.5	36.6	37.7	35.6
15-64	53.5	52.6	54.8	55.8	54.5	56.9	59.6	58.7	60.4
65+	2.5	2.4	2.6	3.3	3.2	3.6	3.8	3.6	4.0
All ages	100.0	100.0	100.0	100.0	100.0	100.0	100.0	100.0	100.0
Dependency ratio	86.9	90.1	82.4	79.2	83.4	75.7	67.8	70.4	65.6

Source: Central Bureau of Statistics.

The proportionate share of the elderly, 65 years and over, also increased between 1971 and 1990 for both males and females.

Between 1971 and 1990, there were also changes in the dependency ratios, which measure the burden of children and the elderly on persons in the working ages. Since the relative share of the working age or productive population has always been higher for females than for males, the burden of dependency has been significantly lower for females than for males. For instance, in 1990, while every 100 males aged 15-64 years had to support 70.4 children and elderly persons, the corresponding ratio for females was only 65.6 dependants. The growing proportion in the 15-64 age group also resulted in a declining dependency ratio between 1971 and 1990 (table 8).

The percentage distribution of the population by broad age groups also differs between

urban and rural areas for both males and females. In the urban areas, the proportionate shares of children aged 0-14 years and of elderly persons 65 years and over are significantly lower and the proportion of persons in working ages 15-64 years is considerably higher than in rural areas for both males and females. The higher proportion of the working-age population in urban than in rural areas reflects, by and large, the preponderance of persons in the working ages in the rural-to-urban migration streams. As a result of the differing patterns, the dependency ratios for both males and females are higher in rural than in urban areas (table 9).

As a result of the changes in the age composition, the number of females in reproductive ages 15-44 years increased by about 60 per cent from 26.4 million in 1971 to 42.2 million in 1990. During this period, the relative share of women aged 15-44 years in the total

Table 9. Percentage distribution of the urban and rural population by three broad age groups and sex, and dependency ratios: 1980 and 1990

Age group	1980				1990			
	Urban		Rural		Urban		Rural	
	Male	Female	Male	Female	Male	Female	Male	Female
0-14	39.4	37.8	43.0	40.1	34.6	32.9	39.2	36:8
15-64	58.3	59.2	53.8	56.2	62.6	63.7	56.9	58.9
65+	2.3	3.0	3.2	3.7	2.8	3.4	3.9	4.3
All ages	100.0	100.0	100.0	100.0	100.0	100.0	100.0	100.0
Dependency ratio	71.5	68.9	85.9	77.9	59.7	57.0	75.7	70.0

Source: Central Bureau of Statistics.

number of women also increased, from 44.0 to 47.0 per cent (table 10). A considerable increase in the number of women in reproductive ages means that, given current patterns of family formation, future annual additions to the total population could be very substantial even if there were to be further declines in fertility rates.

Table 10. Women in the reproductive age group 15-44 years: 1971, 1980 and 1990

Year	Number of women (thousands)		Percentage 15-44 years of all women
	15-44 years	All women	
1971	26 397.1	60 029.2	44.0
1980	32 803.9	73 824.1	44.4
1990	42 246.7	89 872.1	47.0

Source: Central Bureau of Statistics.

(c) Marital status

The numerical and percentage distribution of the population aged 10 years and over by marital status and gender for 1980, 1985 and 1990 is given in table 11. It will be noted that the proportion never married increased between 1980 and 1990 for both males and females, and that in all three years this proportion was reported to be higher among males than females. Further, during the last decade, the percentage of currently married males declined steadily from 55.1 to 53.4 per cent, while that for females fluctuated, although the 1990 proportion is slightly lower than the 1980 proportion. In all years, the proportion widowed as well as divorced was considerably higher among females. In 1990, the proportion widowed among women (9.3 per cent) was approximately six times the corresponding proportion among males.

The higher incidence of widowhood among women is due to a combination of several factors. As noted earlier, mortality among males is higher than among females and this, together with the fact that Indonesian women usually marry men at least several years their senior, results in a higher incidence of widowhood among women. An equally important factor is that the chances of remarriage and thus ending widowhood are much better for widowers than

Table 11. Numerical and percentage distribution of persons 10 years of age and over by marital status and sex: 1980, 1985 and 1990

Marital status and gender	1980		1985		1990	
	Number	Percentage	Number	Percentage	Number	Percentage
Both sexes						
Never married	37 902 288	36.3	46 055 534	38.3	52 119 888	38.6
Currently married	57 371 566	54.9	63 983 871	53.1	72 695 750	53.8
Widowed	6 393 787	6.1	7 477 316	6.2	7 444 980	5.5
Divorced	2 785 987	2.7	2 863 295	2.4	2 778 963	2.1
Total	104 453 628	100.0	120 380 016	100.0	135 039 581	100.0
Male						
Never married	21 585 996	42.0	25 744 417	43.4	29 306 128	43.9
Currently married	28 314 240	55.1	31 889 705	53.8	35 639 314	53.4
Widowed	839 410	1.6	1 016 867	1.7	1 076 769	1.6
Divorced	609 945	1.2	607 226	1.0	664 512	1.0
Total	51 349 591	100.0	59 258 215	100.0	66 666 723	100.0
Female						
Never married	16 316 292	30.7	20 311 117	33.2	22 813 760	33.4
Currently married	29 057 326	54.7	32 094 166	52.5	37 056 436	54.2
Widowed	5 554 377	10.5	6 460 449	10.6	6 368 211	9.3
Divorced	2 176 042	4.1	2 256 069	3.7	2 114 451	3.1
Total	53 104 037	100.0	61 121 801	100.0	68 352 858	100.0

Sources: Central Bureau of Statistics, *Population of Indonesia: Results of the Sub-sample of the 1980 Population Census; Results of the 1985 Intercensal Population Survey;* and *Results of the 1990 Population Census.*

for widows. Similarly, among those divorced, men have a better chance of remarriage than women.

Data from the 1980 and 1990 censuses show that the proportion of males as well as females remaining single was considerably higher in urban than in rural areas. Concomitantly, the proportion currently married was very much higher in rural areas. The incidence of widow-hood and divorce was also higher in rural than in urban areas (table 12).

2. Educational background

As noted earlier, in section B, massive efforts have been made by the Government of Indonesia over the past few decades to expand and develop the national education system. A basic objective behind these efforts has been to provide universal access to schooling at the primary level, in the process eliminating in-equities between urban and rural areas, and among regions and socio-economic classes. Besides the accelerated construction of schools and recruitment and training of teachers, other pragmatic measures include the official abolition of primary school fees, the adoption of a policy of compulsory primary education and the accep-tance of co-education at all levels of formal education as a national policy. There is no dis-crimination based on sex from elementary up to the highest level of schooling. Technical and vocational schools, and training institutes, even those of the Armed Forces, are open to girls and women. Curricula and teaching materials are the same for males and females.

(a) Educational enrolments

As a result of the various measures adop-ted, there has been a rapid increase in school enrolments throughout the country. Available data clearly indicate that women benefited very significantly from the expansion of educational opportunities between 1980 and 1990. At the primary level (ages 7-12 years), the gender gap in educational enrolments which had existed earlier was practically closed in 1980, and by 1990 a slightly higher proportion of girls than boys was enrolled at this level (table 13). Ac-cording to the 1990 population census, among children aged 7-12 years, 95 per cent of the boys and girls in the urban areas and 90 per cent in the rural areas were reported to be attending schools.

It is also evident from table 13 that while at the primary level the female enrolment rate exceeded the male rate, at higher educational levels the participation of females was signifi-cantly lower than that of males; and the higher the level of education, the lower the female participation. The 1990 female enrolment rate was lower than the corresponding male rate by four percentage points at the junior secondary level (ages 13-15), by seven percentage points at the senior secondary level (16-18 years) and by six percentage points at the tertiary level of education (ages 19-24 years), although the gender

Table 12. Percentage distribution of persons aged 10 years and over by marital status and sex in urban and rural areas: 1980 and 1990

Marital status	1980				1990			
	Urban		Rural		Urban		Rural	
	Male	Female	Male	Female	Male	Female	Male	Female
Never married	49.2	38.4	39.9	28.5	49.6	40.6	41.3	30.0
Currently married	48.7	49.2	57.1	56.4	48.5	48.8	55.8	56.7
Widowed	1.2	8.8	1.8	10.9	1.2	7.9	1.8	10.0
Divorced	0.9	3.6	1.2	4.2	0.7	2.7	1.1	3.3
Total	100.0	100.0	100.0	100.0	100.0	100.0	100.0	100.0

Sources: Central Bureau of Statistics, *Population of Indonesia: Results of the Sub-sample of the 1980 Population Census;* and *Results of the 1990 Population Census.*

Table 13. Percentage of school-age group enrolled at any level of schooling by gender: 1980 and 1990

School-age group	1980 census				1990 census			
	Both sexes	Male	Female	Male/ female difference	Both sexes	Male	Female	Male/ female difference
7-12 years	84	84	83	1	92	91	92	−1
13-15 years	60	65	56	9	65	67	63	4
16-18 years	31	39	24	15	41	44	37	7
19-24 years	9	12	5	7	12	15	9	6

Sources: Central Bureau of Statistics, population censuses of 1980 and 1990.

Note: The age groups 7-12, 13-15, 16-18 and 19-24 are the "normal" school-age groups corresponding respectively to primary, junior secondary, senior secondary and tertiary (higher) levels of schooling/education.

disparities in enrolments were considerably reduced between 1980 and 1990.

The data from the 1994 Indonesian Demographic and Health Survey also confirm the pattern of educational enrolments revealed by the 1980 and 1990 census data, in that differences between boys and girls are minimal at the younger age groups (or lower levels of education) but are more marked at the older age groups (or higher levels of education). The 1994 Survey also showed that at all age groups (or all levels of education), the enrolment rates for both males and females were consistently higher in urban than in rural areas. For instance, at ages 7-12 years, or primary level, the enrolment rate for urban females of 97.3 per cent was about eight percentage points higher than the rate of 89.5 per cent reported for rural females. At the junior secondary level (13-15 years), the urban-rural difference in fe-

male enrolment was 21.1 percentage points, while at the senior secondary level (16-18 years) the urban rate of 50.2 per cent was more than double the 22.2 per cent for rural females (table 14).

An important reason for the relatively low participation of girls in secondary education is the non-availability of schools within easy commuting distance. Studies have shown that in Indonesia, the availability of and easy access to schools is highly correlated with the enrolment rates of persons in the secondary school-going age group, and this correlation is significantly stronger for girls than for boys. There are fewer secondary schools than primary schools in the country, and most of the secondary schools are located in urban areas. This would mean that a very high proportion of students from rural areas have to travel long distances to attend secondary schools. For mainly cultural

Table 14. Percentage of the *de jure* household population aged 5-24 years enrolled in school by age group, sex and urban-rural residence: 1994

Age group	Indonesia			Urban			Rural		
	Both sexes	Male	Female	Both sexes	Male	Female	Both sexes	Male	Female
5-6	39.2	36.7	41.7	52.5	50.2	54.6	34.6	32.2	37.0
7-12	91.4	91.2	91.7	96.6	96.1	97.3	89.4	89.3	89.5
13-15	65.4	67.9	62.6	80.7	83.9	77.2	58.5	60.8	56.1
16-18	36.2	39.6	32.9	54.3	58.9	50.2	25.7	29.1	22.2
19-24	10.8	13.3	8.6	21.2	24.4	18.1	4.4	5.8	3.2

Source: Central Bureau of Statistics.

reasons, distance to school is a greater deterrent in the case of females than males; girls are more likely to attend secondary schools if these schools are located within reasonable commuting distance.

Although educational participation rates are lower in rural than in urban areas, available data indicate that between 1980 and 1990, the growth in enrolments was faster in rural than in urban areas (figure 4). The higher growth of enrolments in rural areas has largely been due to a faster expansion of schools in rural areas.

National averages also conceal the marked variation in enrolment ratios across the provinces. Data from the 1980 and 1990 censuses show that enrolment ratios at all levels of education are generally lowest in West Nusa Tenggara, one of the poorest provinces in the country. On the other hand, high enrolment ratios have been reported in respect of North Sumatera, North Sulawesi, Maluku, Aceh, West Sumatera and South Sumatera on account of the role of Christian missions in stressing the value of education and the need for special schools among the Santri (Moslems). The highest enrolment ratios for both males and females in

Figure 4. Percentage of urban and rural population aged 7-24 years attending school, by age group and sex: 1980 and 1990

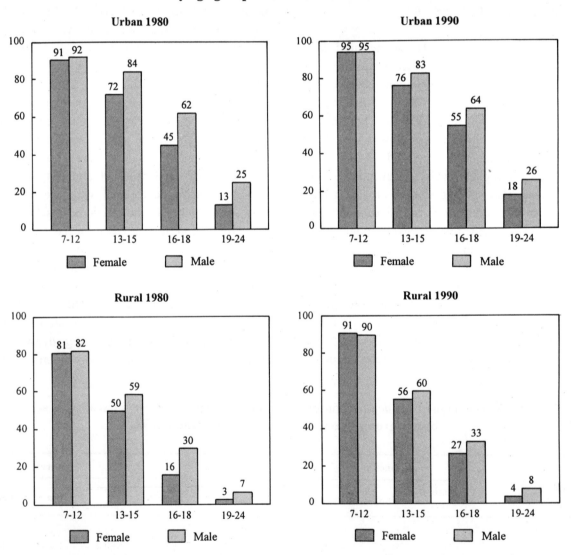

Sources: Central Bureau of Statistics, *Population of Indonesia: Results of the 1980 Population Census;* and *Results of the 1990 Population Census.*

22

1980 and 1990 have been reported for Yogyakarta, perhaps owing to the existence of educational institutions such as Muhammadiyah and the University of Gadjah Mada.

Although around 92 per cent of children in the relevant age group are enrolled in primary schools, a very significant proportion of the children already attending school either drop out before completing the full primary education or take a longer time than needed to complete the primary course. During the period 1983-1985, the drop-out rates averaged 3.5 per cent for the country as a whole but ranged from 2.0 to 7.0 per cent or more across the 27 provinces. Repetition rates also varied widely, from around 6.0 per cent to as much as 15 per cent. In general, rural and remote provinces tend to report higher rates of drop-out and repetition than other areas. In 1992, the primary school completion rate for males (84 per cent) was significantly higher than the 75 per cent estimated for girls. This would mean that drop-out as well as retention is a more serious problem among girls than boys.

According to the 1994 National Socio-economic Survey, a little over 9 per cent of pesons aged 7-24 years had dropped out of the education system at various levels, and this proportion was 9.52 per cent for females and 8.96 per cent for males. The drop-out rate at the primary level was 7.25 per cent for females as against 6.28 per cent for males at the national level. The 1994 Survey data also showed that the primary drop-out rates for both males and females were considerably higher in rural than in urban areas, and that this rate for rural females (9.13 per cent) was more than double the rate of 4.03 per cent reported for urban females. It is also interesting to note that at higher educational levels, the female drop-out rates are either equal to or less than those for males (table 15).

A major cause of primary-school drop-outs in many areas is the inability of families to afford the direct and opportunity costs associated with full-time school attendance by their children. The 1992 National Socio-economic Survey reported that about 50 per cent of persons aged 5-29 years who dropped out of school did so because they did not have enough money. Even though children attending public primary schools are exempted from tuition fees, parents have to provide for uniforms, school materials, contributions and/or supplements for teachers' salaries. Further, while there is no strong son preference in most Indonesian cultures, there is some discrimination against girls, particularly in

Table 15. Percentage of population aged 7-24 years dropping out of the education system at various levels of education, by sex and residence: 1994

Education level	Indonesia			Urban			Rural		
	Both sexes	Male	Female	Both sexes	Male	Female	Both sexes	Male	Female
Primary school	6.76	6.28	7.25	3.62	3.22	4.03	8.55	5.13	9.13
Junior high school									
General	1.51	1.63	1.39	1.25	1.33	1.17	1.66	1.16	1.52
Vocational	0.18	0.18	0.18	0.13	0.15	0.11	0.21	0.13	0.22
Senior high school									
General	0.46	0.51	0.41	0.56	0.62	0.50	0.40	0.29	0.35
Vocational	0.21	0.53	0.19	0.26	0.29	0.23	0.18	0.12	0.16
Diploma I/II	0.03	0.03	0.03	0.04	0.04	0.03	0.02	0.01	0.03
Academy III	0.03	0.03	0.03	0.06	0.06	0.06	0.01	0.01	0.01
University/Diploma IV	0.06	0.07	0.05	0.12	0.14	0.10	0.02	0.02	0.02
Total	9.24	8.96	9.52	6.05	5.85	6.25	9.24	8.96	9.52

Source: Central Bureau of Statistics, *National Socio-economic Survey (SUSENAS), 1994.*

regard to education. A 1991 case study of female-headed households in Cilincing, North Jakarta, found that if parents had limited financial resources for investment in their children's education, they would opt for educating their sons.

Available data also indicate that girls remain under-represented in both general (academic) and vocational secondary schools, despite the existence of special domestic science vocational secondary schools that are also heavily feminized. The proportion of girls in economics secondary schools increased from 44 per cent in 1974 to 61 per cent in 1984/85 and further to 65 per cent in 1990/91. This increase was largely due to the inclusion of more female-oriented specializations, particularly office studies, trade and cooperation. Girls are also concentrated within particular streams. In the general (academic) senior secondary schools, girls are also concentrated within particular streams, especially the language stream, which is the least attractive and stereotypically associated with girls, and are least represented in the science stream. Since streaming is largely based on performance grades, the poorer grades

of girls at senior secondary level partly explain this pattern.

Gender-disaggregated data relating to student enrolments by field of study in institutions of higher learning are not available. However, data relating to persons graduating at this level indicate that girls enrol not only in traditional fields considered suitable for women but also in other areas. In 1993, women constituted 40 per cent of all graduates, and women graduates constituted more than 50 per cent of graduates in humanities and religion (55.5 per cent); fine and applied arts (59.8 per cent); and health and related programmes (57.8 per cent). They also accounted for 48.3 per cent of the graduates in education science; 47.2 per cent of those graduating in the service trades field; 45.1 per cent of mathematics and computer science graduates; 44.2 per cent of business administration graduates; and 41.4 per cent of all graduates in social and behavioural sciences. However, they were very much under-represented in engineering (11.8 per cent), transport and communication (18.6 per cent), and architecture and town planning (23.3 per cent) (table 16).

Table 16. Numerical and percentage distribution of higher education graduates by field of study and sex: 1993

Field of study	Both sexes		Male		Female		Percent-age female
	Number	Percent-age	Number	Percent-age	Number	Percent-age	
Education science	44 084	24.8	22 795	21.4	21 289	29.9	48.3
Humanities and religion	4 237	2.4	1 884	1.8	2 353	3.3	55.5
Fine and applied arts	868	0.5	349	0.3	519	0.7	59.8
Law	14 699	8.3	9 102	8.5	5 597	7.9	38.1
Social and behavioural science	29 230	16.4	17 113	16.1	12 117	17.0	41.4
Business administration	39 641	22.3	22 134	20.8	17 507	24.6	44.2
Communication and documentation	1 538	0.9	995	0.9	543	0.8	35.3
Home economics	–	–	–	–	–	–	–
Service trades	1 109	0.6	586	0.6	523	0.7	47.2
Natural science	1 790	1.0	1 171	1.1	619	0.9	34.6
Mathematics and computer science	1 275	0.7	700	0.7	575	0.8	45.1
Health-related programmes	3 360	1.9	1 418	1.3	1 942	2.7	57.8
Engineering	20 860	11.7	18 402	17.3	2 458	3.5	11.8
Architecture and town planning	1 861	1.0	1 428	1.3	433	0.6	23.3
Trade, craft and industry	270	0.2	200	0.2	70	0.1	25.9
Transport and communication	323	0.2	263	0.2	60	0.1	18.6
Agriculture	12 580	7.1	7 984	7.5	4 596	6.4	36.5
Other and not specified	–	–			–		
Total	177 725	100.0	106 524	100.0	71 201	100.0	40.0

Source: United Nations Educational, Scientific and Cultural Organization, *Statistical Yearbook, 1996.*

(b) *Educational attainment*

As a result of the increasing participation of women in the education system, their level of educational attainment, or the highest level of education achieved, has also been rising steadily. The numerical distribution of persons aged 10 years and over by level of educational attainment as reported in the population censuses of 1980 and 1990 is shown in annex table C.4. The percentage distribution of the same population by educational attainment and sex for two census years as well as for the 1994 National Socio-economic Survey is shown in table 17.

It will be noted from table 17 that the proportion of women with no schooling or incomplete primary education declined from 58.9 per cent in 1980 to 52.9 per cent in 1990 and further to 46.6 per cent in 1994. During this 14-year period there was an increase in the proportions of those completing primary, secondary and tertiary education. Though relatively small, the rate of growth of those completing secondary and higher levels of education has been more marked than that of those completing primary education. It will also be noted from table 17 that the proportion completing any level of education is higher for males than for females. It must be pointed out that according to the 1990 census, 31.8 per cent of males and 31.1 per cent of females aged 10 years and over had not completed primary education; this

relatively high proportion reflects the fairly high drop-out rates at the primary level of education discussed earlier.

The level of educational attainment among males as well as females aged 10 years and over varies between urban and rural areas of the country. According to data from the 1990 population census and the 1994 National Socio-economic Survey, the proportions of the population with no schooling as well as incomplete primary education are considerably lower in the urban areas than in the rural areas for both males and females. For instance, in 1994, the proportion of rural females with no schooling (19.9 per cent) was more than twice the corresponding proportion for urban females (8.7 per cent); and the proportion of rural females with incomplete primary education (35.2 per cent) was one and half times the urban female proportion (22.6 per cent). These disparities reflect those in the availability of schooling facilities as well as the utilization of available facilities between urban and rural areas.

Although the proportion completing primary-level education is higher in rural than in urban areas, the proportions completing junior high school and higher levels of education are considerably higher in urban than in rural areas among both males and females. In 1994, the proportion of urban women completing junior high-school education was 17.1 per cent, or

Table 17. Percentage distribution of persons aged 10 years and over by level of educational attainment and sex: 1980, 1990 and 1994

Level of educational attainment	1980 census			1990 census			1994 SUSENAS	
	Both sexes	Male	Female	Both sexes	Male	Female	Male	Female
No schooling/incomplete primary	55.8	53.2	58.9	47.7	42.4	52.9	37.3	46.6
Primary education	29.2	29.6	28.7	30.4	31.8	29.0	32.9	31.1
Junior high school	8.3	9.0	7.94	10.7	12.1	9.4	13.4	11.0
Senior high school	5.9	7.1	4.5	9.7	11.8	7.7	13.8	9.8
Diploma/academy	0.4	0.5	0.3	0.8	1.0	0.6	1.3	0.8
University	0.3	0.4	0.2	0.7	1.0	0.4	1.4	0.7
Not stated	0.1	0.1	0.1	–	–	–	–	–
Total	100.0	100.0	100.0	100.0	100.0	100.0	100.0	100.0

Sources: Central Bureau of Statistics, *Population of Indonesia: Results of the Sub-sample of the 1980 Population Census; Results of the 1990 Population Census;* and *National Socio-economic Survey (SUSENAS), 1994.*

25

more than twice the proportion of 7.6 per cent recorded for rural women; and the proportion of women completing senior high-school education in urban areas (19.3 per cent) was more than four times the corresponding proportion for rural women. In the urban areas, 1.6 per cent of women aged 10 years and over were university graduates; this proportion among rural women was a mere 0.2 per cent (table 18).

Rising average educational attainment is, of course, reflected in an increasing literacy rate. The literacy rate of the population aged 10 years and over has increased markedly in recent decades and this improvement has been more significant in regard to females than males and in rural areas compared with urban areas. Between 1971 and 1990, the proportion of women 10 years and over who could read and write had increased from 50.0 to 88.6 per cent in urban areas and from 45.1 to 74.1 per cent in rural areas. Over the years, the gap between males and females has also been narrowing, from 33.3 to 7.3 percentage points in urban areas and from 23.1 to 12.5 percentage points in rural areas (table 19).

Although literacy rates have been rising over the years, in 1990 there were, in absolute terms, about 21.5 million illiterates, or persons who could not read and write. Of the 21.5 million illiterate, as many as 14.6 million, or about 68 per cent, were women, and 92 per cent of the illiterate females were aged 25 years and over. The 1990 census also showed that the illiteracy rate increased with age and that at all almost ages the rates for females were considerably higher than for males. For instance, at ages 50 years and over, the female illiteracy rate of 61.8 per cent was almost twice the male rate of 31.8 per cent (table 20).

Table 19. Percentage of population aged 10 years and over able to read and write, by sex and residence: 1971, 1980 and 1990

Year/sex	Indonesia	Urban	Rural
1971 both sexes	60.9		
Male	–	88.3	68.5
Female	–	50.0	45.1
Male-female	–	33.3	23.1
1980 both sexes	71.9	85.0	67.9
Male	80.4	91.7	77.0
Female	63.6	78.4	59.4
Male-female	16.8	13.3	17.6
1990 both sexes	84.1	92.2	80.3
Male	89.6	95.9	86.6
Female	78.7	88.6	74.1
Male-female	10.9	7.3	12.5

Source: Central Bureau of Statistics.

Table 18. Percentage distribution of males aged 10 years and over by level of educational attainment and by urban and rural residence: 1990 census and 1994 National Socio-economic Survey

Level of educational attainment	1990 census				1994 National Socio-economic Survey			
	Urban		Rural		Urban		Rural	
	Male	Female	Male	Female	Male	Female	Male	Female
No schooling	4.3	12.1	13.6	26.3	3.0	8.7	9.8	19.9
Incomplete primary	21.1	23.3	36.8	34.8	20.6	22.6	34.9	35.2
Primary education	28.1	29.3	33.5	28.8	26.6	28.8	36.3	33.3
Junior high school	18.7	16.4	9.0	6.2	18.5	17.1	10.6	7.6
Senior high school	23.0	16.3	6.5	3.7	25.4	19.3	7.5	4.6
Diploma	0.5	0.4	0.2	0.1	0.9	0.7	0.2	0.1
Academy	1.6	1.0	0.2	0.1	1.9	1.2	0.3	0.1
University	2.6	1.2	0.3	0.1	3.3	1.6	0.4	0.2
Total	100.0	100.0	100.0	100.0	100.0	100.0	100.0	100.0

Source: Central Bureau of Statistics, *Population of Indonesia: Results of the 1990 Population Census;* and *National Socio-economic Survey (SUSENAS), 1994.*

**Table 20. Numerical distribution of illiterate persons aged 10 years and over
by age group and sex, and illiteracy rates: 1990 census**

Age gruop	Both sexes		Male		Female	
	Number	Rate	Number	Rate	Number	Rate
10-14	511 644	2.38	265 119	2.40	246 525	2.36
15-19	488 678	2.58	196 527	2.06	292 151	3.11
20-24	840 657	5.21	247 746	3.27	592 911	6.94
25-29	1 489 333	9.53	443 499	5.95	1 045 834	12.81
30-34	1 687 146	12.74	549 156	8.34	1 137 990	17.08
35-39	1 730 564	15.47	580 834	10.03	1 149 730	21.31
40-44	1 820 408	22.53	550 242	13.72	1 270 166	31.20
45-49	2 120 407	28.03	601 495	16.15	1 518 912	39.54
50 and over	10 802 756	47.39	3 492 327	31.83	7 310 429	61.83
Not stated	2 524	57.17	1 084	49.16	1 440	65.16
Total	21 494 117	15.92	6 928 029	10.39	14 566 088	21.31

Source: Central Bureau of Statistics, *Population of Indonesia: Results of the 1990 Population Census.*

The literacy rates also vary across the provinces. In 1990, the female literacy rate ranged from a low of 36.5 per cent in East Timor to a high of 94.0 per cent in Jakarta and 94.8 per cent in North Sulawesi, and was lower than the national average of 78.7 per cent in nine provinces. It was only in North Sulawesi that the female rate almost approximated the male rate, but in several provinces, such as Central Java, Yogyakarta, East Java, West Nusa Tenggara, East Timor, South East Sulawesi and Irian Jaya, the disparity between the male and female literacy rate was considerably higher than the national average of 10.9 percentage points (annex table C.5).

3. Health status

(a) Health services and facilities

The health policy in Indonesia has always recognized the importance of women in different ways: as direct beneficiaries; as mothers and family members; and as health workers, especially as front-line health workers outside the home. Consequently, in addition to the establishment of numerous health centres and subcentres, the government also set up the volunteer-based *posyandu* system of integrated village health posts to provide primary health care to mothers and under five-year-old children through programmes in growth monitoring, nutrition, distribution of vitamin A capsules for children and iron tablets for pregnant women, family planning and education programmes. The system, staffed and managed by community volunteers, has played an important role in extending the provision of health services into the community and has facilitated the spread of family planning, the Expanded Programme of Immunization (EPI) and oral rehydration therapy (ORT) activities.

A very recent development is the village maternity centre, a community-owned facility in which newly placed community midwives work together with traditional birth attendants to provide basic maternity services (antenatal care and normal deliveries). Although still limited to the large provinces, and mostly in Java and Bali, the centres have increased access to maternal health services by about 20 per cent in those provinces. Further, the accelerated training and placement of professional health staff, especially community midwives at the village level, have increased the effectiveness of health services at the primary level.

Several essential services and programmes, particularly related to the health of women and children, are being implemented as an integral part of the primary health care approach.

The Expanded Programme of Immunization, recognized as the key approach in existing child survival services, is an ambititious effort to achieve universal immunization against six childhood diseases: measles, diphtheria, pertusis, tetanus, poliomyelitis and tuberculosis. This programme is carried out primarily through the community health centre which is located in every subdistrict. At least one full-time vaccinator in each centre conducts scheduled visits to pre-arranged sites in the villages. Available data indicate that EPI has achieved at least 80 per cent coverage in 26 of the 27 provinces and in 280 of the 360 districts and cities.

The Indonesian maternal and child health programme attempts to meet the special health needs of mothers, pregnant women and newborn babies through the promotion of attitudinal and behavioural changes conducive to safer delivery and better child health; improvement in the quality of care provided by traditional birth attendants, who continue to play a dominant role in childbirth in the country; referral of high-risk pregnancy cases for professional assistance in delivery; encouragement of breastfeeding; and dietary supplementation to prevent iron deficiency anaemia.

Over the years, the programme has rapidly expanded its network of services and its antenatal care is available to all pregnant women at little cost. However, according to the 1991 Indonesian Demographic and Health Survey, while 80 per cent of the target population had at least one antenatal visit, only 50 per cent had been examined four times in 1991, as recommended by the programme. This Survey also revealed a wide inter-provincial variation in antenatal care coverage, ranging from 32 per cent in Central Sulawesi to 86 per cent in Yogyakarta, owing to socio-cultural factors as well as the availability or accessibility of health facilities.

In order to control the rate of population growth as well as to improve the health and well-being of mothers and their family, the government introduced a nationwide family planning programme in 1970 to encourage couples to limit family size voluntarily. Initially, the programme adopted the slogan "Two children are enough", but today, while continuing to urge voluntary constraint on family size, the movement embraces a wider concept of family welfare by emphasizing "The Small Prosperous Family". The success of the programme is evidenced by the decline in the total fertility rate (TFR) from about 6 children per woman in the 1960s to about 3 children per woman today. Various studies also reveal that about 95 per cent of married women know of at least one method of contraception and that the contraceptive prevalence rate has increased over the years.

An important cause of illness among children under five years is diarrhoea; estimates indicate that around 100,000 infants and children die each year from diarrhoea. The national strategy for control of diarrhoeal diseases emphasizes prevention of mortality from diarrhoeal dehydration rather than reduction of diarrhoeal diseases. As an integral part of this strategy, selected health centres were upgraded to specialize in diarrhoeal disease control through the orientation of volunteer workers, to provide oral rehydration salts, as well as to improve the recording and reporting procedures. Despite intensive efforts to reach children at risk, the oral rehydration therapy strategy does not appear to have been applied effectively in Indonesia. According to a morbidity survey in 10 provinces and routine Ministry of Heath reports from 23 provinces, only about 35 per cent of under five-year-olds with recent diarrhoea had received oral rehydration therapy in 1992.

A major cause of illness among young children is acute respiratory infections (ARI), a rather broad category of diseases including influenza and the common cold, ear and throat infections, bronchitis, bronchiolitis and pneumonia. Available data indicate that ARI account for over 40 per cent of morbidity during infancy and only a slightly lower proportion of the illnesses among children aged 1-4 years. The current strategies include immunization and drug theraopy, and preventive measures to reduce the risk of infection. Indirect methods for combating ARI being pursued in conjunction with the primary health care programmes include good nutrition, improved housing conditions and expansion of health education and facilities.

Since water and sanitation-related diseases cover a wide variety of diseases in the country, the government has accorded priority to the improvement of water supply and sanitation services. However, despite the efforts made, particularly during the International Drinking Water Supply and Sanitation Decade, 1981-1990, a large segment of the population throughout the country still lacks access to both clean and sufficient drinking water and adequate waste disposal facilities.

The implementation of various public health programmes has, by and large, involved women in their dual role as consumers and active participants. About 46 per cent of all para-medical personnel are women, engaged mostly as midwives and nurses, dentists, pharmacists, nutritionists etc., and about 29 per cent of the medical doctors are also women with a position in the health centres. Available data indicate an increasing trend in the number of female health workers in every field, in both technical and administrative areas. In recognition of the important role that women play in the implementation of health care in general and of village health programmes in particular, the Family Welfare Movement was awarded the Maurice Pate Award as well as the World Health Organization's Sasakawa Prize in 1988.

In recent years, considerable progress has been made in extending modern health care to the poor. According to the 1987 National Socio-economic Survey, the proportion of poor people using some kind of modern health facility when they fall ill increased from less than 40 per cent in the late 1970s to over 50 per cent at the time of the Survey. During this period, there has also been an increase in the use of modern treatment by the poor, from 41 to 52 per cent in rural Java. The use of health centres, including subcentres, increased from 17 per cent in 1978 to 31 per cent in 1987, with similar increases reported in respect of rural outer islands. It has, however, to be noted that while access to services has increased significantly in quantitative terms, there is still considerable scope for improving the quality of the services provided in terms of availability of drugs and qualified medical staff, mostly in poor areas.

Owing to the low levels of education, particularly among women in rural areas, there is inadequate understanding and insufficient awareness of health problems among the people. Superstitious beliefs in rural and remote areas also inhibit attempts to improve the health status through increasing availability and utilization of modern health facilities. Communication problems due to the geography of Indonesia also hinder the implementation of health programmes.

(b) Morbidity patterns

Available data and information clearly show that the most common diseases, among both males and females, are infections of the respiratory organs, including tuberculosis, infections of the skin, diarrhoea, malaria, nutritional disorders and eye diseases. This general pattern of morbity has been observed in rural as well as urban areas.

It is also generally established that infancy and early childhood are the unhealthiest periods of life prior to old age, and that in Indonesia the relative share of diseases among infants and children is greatly out of proportion to their share of the total population. Estimates show that the under five-year-olds, who constitute about 12 per cent of the total population, contribute to more than 25 per cent of the morbidity cases in the country. Each child under five years old contracted an average of four diseases per year, the main diseases being respiratory infections, skin infections, diarrhoea and nutritional deficiencies.

According to the 1994 Demographic and Health Survey, about 10 per cent of children under five years of age had attacks of coughing with rapid breathing during the two weeks preceding the Survey, indicating that these children were suffering from pneumonia and needed hospitalization. The Survey also showed that the prevalence rate was highest (13.3 per cent) among children aged 6-11 months but decreased with increasing age. The prevalence rate was higher for males (10.7 per cent) than for females (9.3 per cent) and in rural areas (10.3 per cent) than in urban areas (9.3 per cent).

Studies have shown that diarrhoea is the most common illness during the first two years of life. The 1991 Demographic and Health Survey reported that the overall percentage of children with diarrhoea was 4.0 per cent in the 24 hours preceding the Survey investigation, and 11 per cent during the two weeks preceding the Survey. The incidence rate was about the same in both rural and urban areas and among males as well as females, but there was marked variation between the provinces, ranging from 1-2 per cent in East Kalimantan, East Nusa Tenggara, Yogyakarta and East Java to 6-8 per cent in South East Sulawesi, West Nusa Tenggara, West Kalimantan and West Java.

Diarrhoea and skin diseases are also the second and third most important causes of morbidity among children aged one to four years, with skin diseases being responsible for about 15 per cent and diarrhoea for 11 per cent of morbidity in this age group. Bronchitis, asthma and other respiratory ailments account for about 13 per cent of the morbidity in the one-to-four age group. It is also evident from table 21 that there are only a few major differences in the causal patterns of infant and child morbidity, with 66-70 per cent of total morbidity in both groups being accounted for in

three disease categories: accute respiratory infections, diarrhoea, and skin infections. Malaria and nervous system disorders are more important causes of morbidity among toddlers than among infants.

Among the important risk factors related to respiratory tract infections are inadequate nutrition and overcrowded living conditions, while the major causes of diarrhoea and skin infections are poor personal hygiene and inadequate sanitation or insanitary excreta disposal and poor drainage systems.

A systematic study of the nutritional status of children in Indonesia is hampered by the availability of comprehensive investigations. However, available information suggests that undernourishment is a fairly serious problem among children. The 1986 and 1987 National Socio-economic Surveys provide the most extensive data, since each child under age five years in the sampled households was weighed and its nutritional status, based on weight for age, estimated. These anthropometric measurements of 20,000-30,000 children living in all provinces indicate that in 1987, just under half of the young children in the country were adequately nourished. About 40 per cent suffer from

Table 21. Major causes of infant and child morbidity: 1986

Major cause	Under 1 year			1-4 years		
	Rate[a/]	Percent-age	Cumulative percentage	Rate[a/]	Percent-age	Cumulative percentage
Acute respiratory infections (ARI)	70.2	42.4	42.4	73.8	40.6	40.6
Diarrhoea	25.0	15.1	57.5	20.6	11.4	52.0
Skin infections	20.1	12.2	69.7	26.3	14.5	66.5
Bronchitis, asthma, other respiratory infections	13.3	8.0	77.7	12.9	7.1	73.6
Nervous system disorders	7.5	4.5	82.2	11.5	6.3	79.9
Tuberculosis, diphtheria, pertusis, measles	6.8	4.2	86.4	5.4	3.0	82.9
Malaria	2.6	1.6	88.0	7.9	4.4	87.3
Others	20.2	12.0	100.0	23.1	12.7	100.0
All causes	165.7	100.0	–	181.5	100.0	–

Source: Cited in United Nations Children's Fund, *Situation Analysis of Children and Women in Indonesia* (Jakarta, 1989).

[a/] Per thousand persons in the age group.

mild undernourishment and approximately one child out of nine is moderately or severely undernourished. Information for recent years indicates that boys are more malnourished than girls and that malnourishment is highest among rural boys (55.5 per cent) and lowest among urban girls (33.4 per cent).

Other nutritional problems include vitamin A deficiency, iodine deficiency disorders and nutritional anaemia. Indonesian women are highly prone to iron deficiency anaemia, particularly during pregnancy. Data from the 1992 Household Health Survey indicate that although nutritional anaemia has declined in recent years, about 64 per cent of all pregnant women were suffering from anaemia in 1992. Most anaemia among pregnant and non-pregnant adult women is largely due to the lack of iron-rich foods during adolescence, Nutritional anaemia is also considered a major cause of maternal death since it tends to aggravate other risks associated with pregnancy, such as pre-eclampsia, eclampsia, ante partum haemorrhage and sepsis.

As noted earlier, a woman's nutritional status is determined by her diet during childhood and adolescent years. In low-income families with limited resources, intra-familiar food distribution is often influenced by socio-cultural values that generally give priority to men and children in the matter of food intake. Consequently, girls generally receive less food than their male siblings. Further, food taboos stemming from cultural beliefs are commonly imposed in many parts of the country on pregnant and lactating women, thus depriving them of vital nutritional intake during a critical period. For example, in Java and Sumatera, pregnant women usually avoid eating certain fruits such as pineapple and durian as well as certain kinds of fish, mutton and yeast, which are rich sources of vitamins and proteins and therefore important for a healthy pregnancy.

(c) Mortalility levels and trends

A systematic analysis of levels, patterns and trends of mortality in Indonesia is to a large extent hampered by the lack of accurate and up-to-date data and information. Data from the country's vital registration system are subject

to gross under-registration, while a substantial proportion of deaths which have occurred are not reported in surveys owing to problems of recall lapse. Most estimates of mortality levels have been derived using childhood mortality estimates based on survey and census data as well as model life tables. However, no firm conclusion could be made regarding the pattern of mortality in Indonesia on account of doubts raised about the quality of the basic data, such as under-reporting of deaths, under-enumeration of the population and age misreporting.

(i) Infant mortality

Estimates based on data from censuses and surveys indicate a dramatic decline in the infant mortality rate per 1,000 live births from 142 based on 1971 census data to 112 based on 1980 census data, and further to 70 based on 1990 data. (The officially estimated infant mortality rate based on 1990 census data is 63 per 1,000 live births). Estimates derived from the Indonesian Demographic and Health Survey data show that the infant mortality rate continued to decline to 68 in 1991 and 57 in 1994 (figure 5). The declining trend in the infant mortality rate is also confirmed by recent estimates prepared by the United Nations, according to which Indonesia's infant mortality rate

Figure 5. Estimates of infant mortalily rate based on census and survey data: 1971-1994

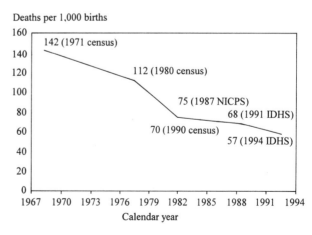

Deaths per 1,000 births

Source: **Central Bureau of Statistics (CBS), Indonesia** and State Ministry of Population/National Family Planning Coordinating Board (NFPCB), and Ministry of Health (MOH) and Macro International Inc. (MI), 1995. *Indonesia Demographic and Health Survey, 1994.* Calverton, Maryland: CBS and MI.

had been more than halved, from 160 in 1950-1955 to 58 in 1990-1995.

Although estimates based on various sources indicate that the infant mortality rate has been declining rapidly over the years, Indonesia still lags behind many of its Asian neighbours, particularly in East and South-East Asia, in the level of the infant mortality rate. According to United Nations estimates, Indonesia's infant mortality rate of 58 per 1,000 live births in 1990-1995 was over 11 times the rate for Singapore (5), over 6 times that for Brunei Darussalam (9), over 4 times that for Malaysia (13) and considerably higher than the rates for Thailand (32), the Philippines (40) and China (44). Further, infant mortality continues to account for over 20 per cent of all deaths in Indonesia every year.

The infant mortality rate varies markedly across the provinces; in 1990, the estimated rate for West Nusa Tenggara (145) was over three times that of 40 in Jakarta and 42 in Yogyakarta. While these are extreme cases, it is worth noting that Yogyakarta and West Nusa Tenggara were also the two provinces with the lowest and highest rates respectively in 1980 as well. In 1990, there 12 provinces in which the rate was significantly higher than the national average of 71 per 1,000 live births (annex table C.6). By and large, poor and remote provinces experience high infant mortality rates, but high levels of infant mortality are not necessarily associated with poverty. For instance, West Nusa Tenggara and East Nusa Tenggara are very poor areas, but the rate in West Nusa Tenggara is almost double that in East Nusa Tenggara. The rate of the church in instilling a sense of cleanliness, health and nutrition has been mentioned as an important factor relating to the lower infant mortality rate in East Nusa Tenggara.

The mortality rate is also significantly higher among male infants than among female infants and this gender disparity is reported in respect of all provinces. In 1990, the female infant mortality rate was very low in Jakarta (35) and Yogyakarta (36) and highest in West Nusa Tenggara; it was higher than the national average in nine provinces (annex table C.6).

Accurate and up-to-date data on the cause of infant mortality are not available. However, fairly comprehensive information is available from a 1985/86 health survey of 50,000 households conducted by the Department of Health covering 63 districts in seven provinces (Yogyarta, Bali, North Sulawesi, Bengkulu, West Kalimantan, Maluku and West Nusa Tenggara) selected to represent the range of provincial estimates of infant mortality rates in 1980. According to this survey, four main cause categories (tetanus, perinatal causes, diarrhoea and ARI) together accounted for more than two thirds (67.7 per cent) of all infant deaths in 1986. About 28 per cent of all infant deaths have been caused by immunizable diseases (tetanus, measles, diphtheria and whooping cough) while perinatal causes accounted for close to 1 in 5 deaths (table 22). Most of the perinatal and congenital deaths are probably a consequence of poor maternal health and nutritional deficiency during pregnancy, possibly combined with inadequate care at the time of delivery.

(ii) Child mortality

Mortality among children aged one to four years is estimated to have declined from about 22 per thousand children in 1965 to 18 per thousand in 1980 and to about 9 per thousand in 1990. In other words, the child mortality rate had declined by about 59 per cent over a 25-year period. This decline is slower than that recorded in respect of the infant mortality rate and in this respect Indonesia's experience differs from that of many other countries in the region. Further, despite the progress made in reducing the child mortality rate, child mortality accounts for about 8 per cent of all deaths in Indonesia every year.

According to the 1985/86 Household Health Survey, diarrhoea and the immunizable diseases (measles, diphtheria, whooping cough and tetanus) together accounted for 55.6 per cent of all deaths in the 1-4 age group, while ARI was the cause of another 8.4 per cent of childhood mortality. Thus, the vaccine-preventable diseases plus diarrhoea and ARI accounted for nearly two thirds of early child deaths. The other significant causes were malaria and accidents (table 23).

Table 22. Distribution of infant deaths by underlying cause: 1986

Underlying cause	Percentage of infant deaths	Rate per 100,000 live births	Estimated number of infant deaths, 1985
Tetanus	19.3	1 383.5	73 300
Perinatal causes	18.4	1 320.6	69 900
Diarrhoea	15.6	1 119.4	59 200
ARI (including bronchitis and asthma)	14.4	1 031.3	54 700
Measles	7.5	540.8	28 500
Nervous system disorders	5.6	402.5	21 300
Congenital disorders	4.2	301.8	16 000
Diphtheria, whooping cough	1.0	75.5	3 800
Anaemia, malnutrition	1.0	75.5	3 800
Other and undetermined	13.0	930.7	49 400
All causes	100.0	7 181.6	380 000

Source: Cited in United Nations Children's Fund, *Situation Analysis of Children and Women in Indonesia* (Jakarta, 1989).

Table 23. Major underlyng causes of death among children 1-4 years: 1986

Underlying cause	Rate per 100,000 children 1-4 years	Percentage of all child deaths	Cumulative percentage	Estimated number of deaths, 1985
Diarrhoea	278.4	26.4	26.4	47 800
Measles, diphtheria, pertussis	291.5	27.6	54.0	50 000
Acute respiratory infections (ARI)	88.4	8.4	62.4	15 200
Malaria	55.7	5.3	67.7	9 600
Accidents, injuries	52.4	5.0	72.7	9 000
Nervous system disorders	49.1	4.7	77.4	8 500
Anaemia, malnutrition, avitaminosis	26.2	2.5	79.9	4 500
Bronchitis, asthma	26.2	2.5	82.4	4 500
Tetanus	16.4	1.6	84.0	2 900
All other causes/undetermined	170.5	16.0	100.0	29 000
All causes	1 054.8	100.0	–	181 000

Source: Cited in United Nations Children's Fund, *Situation Analysis of Children and Women in Indonesia* (Jakarta, 1989).

According to the 1992 Household Health Survey, diarrhoea and ARI are the major causes of child mortality, with ARI being the single biggest killer in the first year and diarrhoea the major killer in the second to fifth years. The immuno-preventable diseases accounted for about 10 per cent of child mortality (figure 6). Malnutrition was not reported to be a cause of child death in the 1992 survey; malnutrition is rarely certified as a cause of death.

(iii) Maternal mortality

In Indonesia, as in most developing countries, reliable and up-to-date data and information on maternal mortality are not available. Various studies conducted in the country during the past three decades have reported maternal mortality rates ranging from 150 to 720 per 100,000 live births. For instance, the 1980 Household Health Survey conducted in six provinces (including East, West and Central Java) reported an overall rate of 150 maternal deaths per 100,000 live births. The 1986 Household Health Survey covering seven provinces (mostly outside Java) gave an overall rate of 450 but ranging between 130 and 780 across the seven provinces. The most recent estimate of the maternal mortality rate based on the data of the 1994 Demographic and Health Survey is 390 maternal

Figure 6. Major cause of child death by age group: 1992

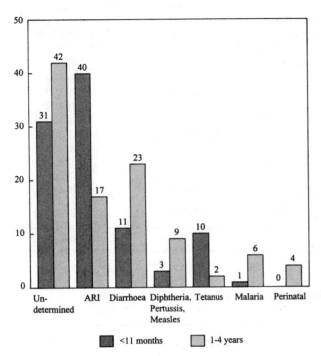

Source: Government of Indonesia.

deaths per 100,000 live births. Smaller studies have tended to report relatively higher maternal mortality rates. For instance, a reproductive age mortality study conducted in Bali during the period 1980-1982 found a maternal mortality rate of 761 per 100,000 live births.

The wide variation in reported rates is due to differences in definition, data collection methods, sample size and analytical techniques, as well as to a weak monitoring and evaluation component of maternal and child health programmes. To some extent the marked variations also reflect differences within the country. Nevertheless, compared with most other Association of South East Asian Nations (ASEAN) countries, even the lowest estimate of the Indonesian maternal mortality rate is high, though not greatly out of line with estimates for a number of other countries in Asia and Africa.

It is conventional to classify the causes of maternal mortality into three categories: direct obstetric causes related to complications of delivery or pregnancy or their management; indirect obstetric causes or deaths resulting from the aggravation of some existing condition by pregnancy or delivery; and unrelated causes or

deaths occurring to women who have been pregnant within the previous 42 days but which are not related, directly or indirectly, to pregnancy or delivery. Although, globally, around 80 per cent of maternal deaths are due to direct obstetric causes such as haemorraghia, toxaemia, infection (sepsis), obstructed labour and abortion, in Indonesia, a 1977-1980 study covering 12 teaching hospitals found direct obstetric causes to be responsible for 94.4 per cent and indirect causes for another 4.6 per cent of maternal deaths occurring in the participating hospitals. A World Bank study reported that in 1992, haemorrhage, infection and toxaemia together accounted for an estimated 75-85 per cent of all cases of maternal mortality in Indonesia.

An important reason for the high rate of maternal mortality as well as the very high proportion of maternal deaths due to direct obstetric causes is the fact that a very large proportion of births in Indonesia are delivered at home, mostly assisted by traditional birth attendants. According to recent data from the 1994 Demographic and Health Survey, 82.2 per cent of all live births in the five years preceding the Survey were delivered either at the mother's home (70.6 per cent), or at other homes (6.2 per cent), or at the home of the midwife (5.4 per cent). Data from various surveys also indicate that only about 32-36 per cent of the deliveries are attended to or assisted by trained health personnel, such as a doctor or a midwife, and the rest by non-trained personnel, such as a traditional birth attendant or a relative (table 24).

It is also evident from table 24 that the percentage of deliveries taking place wtih the assistance of a qualified doctor is very much higher in urban than in rural areas. Yet, about two thirds of urban deliveries are supervised by a trained midwife. Studies have shown that women prefer midwives to doctors for several reasons, such as convenience, low cost, flexible payment arrangements, more attention given by midwife than doctor, and the after-care services offered. Further, midwives know their patients well and are willing to attend to the delivery at the mother's home. In the rural areas, the vast majority of births are attended to by traditional

Table 24. Percentage distribution of live births by type of assistance during delivery and residence: 1987, 1991 and 1994

Type of assistance	1987 National Indonesia Contraceptive Prevalence Survey			1991 Demographic and Health Survey			1994 Demographic and Health Survey		
	Indonesia	Urban	Rural	Indonesia	Urban	Rural	Indonesia	Urban	Rural
Doctor	4.0	10.3	1.6	2.4	6.5	0.7	2.7	7.3	1.0
Midwife	32.3	58.7	22.5	29.3	58.2	17.5	33.8	66.3	21.5
Traditional birth attendant	60.7	30.1	72.4	63.7	34.2	75.5	59.5	25.2	72.4
Relative	1.7	0.5	2.1	3.8	0.7	5.1	3.2	0.9	4.0
Other	0.9	0.4	1.1	0.5	0.4	0.5	0.4	0.2	0.6
None	0.2	0.0	0.2	0.3	0.1	0.6	0.4	0.1	0.5
Total	100.0	100.0	100.0	100.0	100.0	100.0	100.0	100.0	100.0

Sources: Central Bureau of Statistics, *National Indonesia Contraceptive Prevalence Survey, 1987; Indonesia Demographic and Health Survey, 1991;* and *Indonesia Demographic and Health Survey, 1994.*

birth attendants who are generally untrained but are highly esteemed for their knowledge of traditional customs concerning birth and the massages they give the mother and the baby.

(iv) Life expectancy

The improvement in the health status of the population is reflected in the increase in life expectancy at birth. Estimates based on the 1980 and 1990 census data indicate that life expectancy at birth for females increased from 54.0 in 1980 to 61.5 in 1990, while male life expectancy increased from 50.9 to 58.1 during the same period. Estimates also indicate that there has been further improvement, with the value for females increasing to 64.9 and for males to 61.2 in 1994. Thus, female life expectancy has consistently been higher than male life expectancy (annex table C.7).

The national average, however, conceals the significant variation in life expectancy between various provinces. In 1994, life expectancy was highest (71.3 years for females and 67.3 years for males) in Jakarta, and lowest (54.3 years for females and 51.2 years for males) in West Nusa Tenggara (annex table C.7).

D. WOMEN IN FAMILY LIFE

1. Indonesian family system

(a) Family type

A major socio-cultural feature of the Indonesian people is the pluralism in family or kinship system which varies among the ethnic groups. All types of kinship system – bilateral parental, patrilineal or matrilineal, or variations thereof – are represented in the Indonesian society. However, the most prominent family patterns are those based on bilateral descent, being prevalent particularly among the Javanese, Sudanese and Madurese. The next most common descent system is the patrilineal pattern, followed by the Balinese, the Batakanese of North Sumatera and also the Chinese. The Minangkabau of West Sumatera is one of the few groups in the world maintaining a matrilineal system of inheritance.

Although official statistics on family types are not available, it is generally accepted that a large number of Indonesian families, particularly those in rural areas, belong to the category of limited extended family, which usually consists of husband and wife, their unmarried children and the surviving parent of the husband or wife. In Bali, an extended family is formed by a number of nuclear families living in a walled compound, with one common family temple. Among the Dayaks of Kalimantan, several nuclear families live in a long-house under the leadership of a "family head" assisted by a council of elders. In Java, families may remain extended for many years, especially if they are poor.

However, the nuclear structure is becoming increasingly common, particularly in the urban areas. A 1990 study relating to working and non-working mothers in Jakarta revealed that about two thirds of the families in this city were of the nuclear type. Available data also indicate that urban nuclear families, particularly those in the slums, often include close and distant relatives who come to the cities in search of a better life. The trend towards nuclearization of families is also evident from an increase in the proportion of small-sized families. It is clear from figure 7 that the proportionate share of households with fewer than five members increased substantially between 1980 and 1990.

Figure 7. Changes in average household size between 1980 and 1990

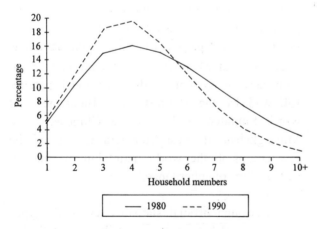

Source: Central Bureau of Statistics.

Unlike many other Asian countries, there is less rigid division of labour within the household between men and women in Indonesia. However, women continue to shoulder the major share of household chores and responsibilities,

and several studies have shown that women usually work longer hours than men. Socio-cultural values and customs also tend to accord priority to men and children in the distribution of food within the family, although this practice is reported to be on the decline. Women also generally occupy a low status in patrilineal families, in which the birth of a son is regarded as imperative to ensure the continuity of the family lineage and religious tradition. Nevertheless, for various reasons women tend to play an important role in decisions about the allocation of household resources, including both savings and consumption.

(b) Household heads

In Indonesia, traditional social conventions as well as present-day administrative arrangements have placed men as heads of households; a woman is seldom recognized as the head in any household with an adult male member. This is largely because men have to spend significantly more time than women in formal social and religious activities, and are also the major decision makers in the community. Irrespective of her role in the household affairs, as well as her contribution to the maintenance of the household, there have to be unusual circumstances for a woman to be classified as head of household in surveys and census enumerations. By formal definition, a woman is considered to be the household head if (a) she is single, widowed or divorced and there are no adult males in her household; or (b) she is currently married but her husband has been away from home for six months or longer. In cases where a man has more than one wife, he is counted as head of his first wife's household only.

Data from censuses and surveys indicate that the number of female-headed households in the country increased from about 4.3 million in 1980 to 5.3 million in 1990 and further to 5.4 million in 1994. These data also show that practically the entire growth in female-headed households has taken place in the urban areas, where such households more than doubled, from about 857 thousand in 1980 to over 1.9 million in 1994, while in the rural areas there appears to have been a decline in these households, from 3.7 million in 1990 to about 3.5 million in 1994.

Consequently, the proportionate share of female-headed households in the total number of households increased from 19.7 per cent in 1980 to 35.9 per cent in 1994 in urban areas, and declined from 80.3 to 64.1 per cent in the rural areas during the same period (table 25).

Although the female-headed households increased in absolute terms in Indonesia between 1980 and 1994, there was a decline in these households in relative or proportionate terms from 14.2 to 12.6 per cent owing to the rapid rate of total household formation during the same period. While in the rural areas, the relative share of female-headed households decreased from 14.4 to 12.2 per cent, it remained more or less stable at 13.5 per cent in the urban areas during the 14-year period 1980-1994 (table 26).

Data from the 1980 and 1990 censuses also show that in both urban and rural areas, while the vast majority of male household heads were married, the majority of female households were either widowed or divorced. In 1990, female household heads who were married constituted only 11.8 per cent of all female household heads in rural areas and 13.6 per cent in urban areas (table 27). By and large, women become heads of their households on the death of their husbands.

According to the 1994 National Socio-economic Survey, while nearly 69 per cent of all male household heads in the country were under 50 years of age, the majority (59.8 per cent) of all female household heads were over 50 years of age. The Survey also showed that the proportion of female household heads aged 50 years and over was significantly higher in rural areas (62.9 per cent) compared with urban areas (54.3 per cent) (table 28).

The proportion of households headed by women varies markedly across the various provinces. According to the 1994 National Socio-economic Survey, this proportion was lowest (5.4 per cent) in Iriyan Jaya, while it ranged between 6.0 and 10.0 per cent in 12 other provinces; and was higher than the national average (12.6 per cent) in eight other provinces, being highest in West Sumatera (19.9 per cent) followed by Yogyakarta (19.2 per cent) (see annex table D.1). The relatively high proportion of female-headed households in West Sumatera could be explained in terms of the migrant tradition (*merantau*) among the Minangkabau males. West Sumatera is among the provinces with very heavy out-migration and it has been the custom for the wife to assume de facto headship of the household in the absence of the husband. The relatively high proportion of female-headed households in Yogyakarta is due to the fact that a substantial number of young educated women live by themselves in this city.

Table 26. Female-headed households as percentage of total households by residence: 1980, 1990 and 1994

Residence	1980	1990	1994
Indonesia	14.2	13.5	12.6
Urban	13.5	13.7	13.5
Rural	14.4	13.1	12.2

Source: Central Bureau of Statistics, censuses of population and housing, 1980 and 1990; and *National Socio-economic Survey (SUSENAS), 1994.*

Table 25. Numerical and percentage distribution of female-headed households by residence: 1980, 1990 and 1994

Residence	1980		1990		1994	
	Number	Percentage	Number	Percentage	Number	Percentage
Indonesia	4 344 912	100.0	5 267 333	100.0	5 434 048	100.0
Urban	857 045	19.7	1 596 692	30.3	1 949 729	35.9
Rural	3 487 867	80.3	3 670 641	69.7	3 484 319	64.1

Source: Central Bureau of Statistics, censuses of population and housing, 1980 and 1990; and *National Socio-economic Survey (SUSENAS), 1994.*

**Table 27. Percentage distribution of male and female household heads
by marital status and residence: 1980 and 1990**

Residence/marital status	1980		1990	
	Male	Female	Male	Female
Urban				
Unmarried	3.9	8.6	7.7	14.8
Married	94.1	18.2	90.0	13.6
Divorced	0.6	15.7	0.7	13.8
Widowed	1.4	57.5	1.6	57.8
Total	100.0	100.0	100.0	100.0
Rural				
Unmarried	1.3	2.6	4.0	3.8
Married	96.0	13.0	93.1	11.8
Divorced	0.7	18.1	0.8	17.3
Widowed	1.9	66.2	2.0	67.1
Total	100.0	100.0	100.0	100.0

Source: Central Bureau of Statistics, population censuses of 1980 and 1990.

Table 28. Percentage distribution of household heads by age group, sex and residence: 1994

Age group	Indonesia		Urban		Rural	
	Male	Female	Male	Female	Male	Female
<20	0.39	1.90	0.55	3.84	0.30	0.81
20-24	3.00	3.85	3.32	8.25	2.84	1.38
25-29	9.88	3.91	9.64	4.98	10.00	3.31
30-34	14.73	4.91	15.35	4.96	14.43	5.01
35-39	16.30	6.86	16.61	6.14	16.14	7.25
40-44	14.08	8.66	14.95	8.45	13.65	8.78
45-49	10.61	10.02	10.25	9.09	10.79	10.54
50-54	10.11	14.44	10.00	13.46	10.17	14.98
55-59	6.90	12.16	6.59	12.00	7.06	12.25
60+	13.99	33.22	12.74	28.82	14.61	35.68
Total	100.00	100.00	100.00	100.00	100.00	100.00

Source: Central Bureau of Statistics, *National Socio-economic Survey (SUSENAS), 1994.*

2. Family formation

(a) Marriage patterns

In Indonesia, socio-cultural norms and values have traditionally favoured universal and early marriage for both males and females. With the exception of religious priests and nuns, who are required to be celibate, other persons who opt to remain unmarried are regarded as socially deviant and maladjusted. The universality of marriage is reflected in the very high proportions (98.0 per cent of females and 96.6 per cent of males) reported to be ever married before 45 years of age at the 1990 census.

Traditionally, parents have been responsible for arranging marriages for their children, and have most often been involved in arranging the marriages of their daughters shortly after puberty; boys have been under less pressure to marry early. Generally, the first marriages are between spouses who are strangers to one another and arranged through the negotiation of an intermediary, and with reference to social rank and class, and also (in the case of Muslims) to one's own stream of Islam. While the well-to-do and upper classes often prefer certain cross-cousin marriages to strengthen kindred ties, among the ordinary peasantry it is sometimes considered preferable not to marry among relatives in order to avoid straining familial bonds resulting from the high divorce rate. Young people have been bound by the wishes of their parents in respect to marriage, and it has been widely believed that a marriage without parental approval will not be a happy marriage.

Early marriage for girls has been an important feature of the marriage pattern in Indonesia and the prevalence of this practice is attested to by data from censuses and surveys. At the 1980 census, about 43 per cent of all ever-married women aged 10 years and over reported that their first marriage took place when they were 10-16 years old, while another about 25 per cent married for the first time when they were 17-18 years old. Thus more than two thirds of the ever-married women contracted their first marriage when they were under 19 years of age. However, the proportion of females being married off at a relatively young age has been declining over the years and, according to the 1994 Demographic and Health Survey, 56 per cent of all ever-married women reported that they were below 19 years of age when they married for the first time (table 29).

Available data also indicate that the incidence of early female marriages is significantly higher in rural than in urban areas. The proportion of ever-married women aged 10 years and over who reported being married for the first time when they were below 19 years of age was 70.4 per cent in rural areas and 58.9 per cent in urban areas, according to the 1980 census, and 60.7 per cent in rural areas and

46.0 per cent in urban areas, according to the 1994 Demographic and Health Survey (table 29).

There is also a marked variation in the incidence of early marriages for females across the 27 provinces of the country. Data from the 1980 and 1990 population censuses, as well as from the 1994 Survey, confirm that the proportion of women marrying at ages 10-16 years was lowest in East Nusa Tenggara, Bali, Maluku and North Sulawesi, and highest in West Java, East Java and South Kalimantan. For instance, in 1994, while nearly 27 per cent of all ever-married women aged 10 years and over in the country were reported as having married at ages 10-16 years, this proportion ranged from about 4 to 9 per cent in East Nusa Tenggara, Bali, Maluku and North Sulawesi, and from 32 to 39 per cent in South Kalimantan, East Java and West Java. The 1994 Survey also showed that the proportion of women marrying at ages below 19 was also low (18-26 per cent) in East Nusa Tenggara, Bali, Maluku and North Sulawesi, and high (63-70 per cent) in South Kalimantan, East Java and West Java (annex table D.2).

Several reasons have been advanced to explain the marked inter-provincial differences in age at first marriage of females. For instance, the relatively high proportion of females marrying at young ages in Java is largely due to the socio-cultural traditions of the Javanese and Sudanese ethnic groups. Studies have shown that most Javanese and Sudanese believe that a girl who is not married by age 17 is an "old maid" and a disgrace to her parents. This belief

Table 29. Percentage distribution of ever-married women aged 10 years and over by age at first marriage and residence: 1980, 1990 and 1994

Age at first marriage	1980 census			1990 census			1994 Demographic and Health Survey		
	Indonesia	Urban	Rural	Indonesia	Urban	Rural	Indonesia	Urban	Rural
10-16	43.4	35.6	45.4	37.0	30.0	39.9	26.9	20.8	29.8
17-18	24.6	23.3	25.0	25.1	22.5	26.2	29.1	25.2	30.9
19-24	24.6	31.5	22.9	31.9	38.3	29.3	38.1	44.3	35.2
25+	7.4	9.6	6.7	5.9	9.1	4.6	5.9	9.7	4.1
Total	100.0	100.0	100.0	100.0	100.0	100.0	100.0	100.0	100.0

Sources: Central Bureau of Statistics, population censuses of 1980 and 1990; and *Indonesia Demographic and Health Survey, 1994.*

is also reinforced by the prevailing religious views, which encourage parents to marry off their daughters soon after puberty. Early marriage for girls is also very common among the poor people; the sooner a girl marries the better for the parents, as they will be relieved of the burden of supporting their daughter. The poor do not see any other option for overcoming poverty except to let their daughters marry as soon as possible.

The low prevalence of early marriage for girls in East Nusa Tenggara, Maluku and North Sulawesi is due to the influence of Christian missionaries in stressing the importance of education for girls, thereby delaying their marriage. In Bali, a predominantly Hindu province, the religious writing *Manawadharmacastra* clearly states that it is better for a female not to marry if a suitable husband is not available. Hence, parents delay the marriage of their daughters until they can find appropriate spouses.

A recent study on marriage patterns in Java based on data from the 1991 Demographic and Health Survey revealed that 70 per cent of ever-married women in Java married early or before age 20, with the age at first marriage increasing from the older to the younger cohort. The study also revealed that the proportion of women who married early was higher in rural than in urban areas, among those with no education or little education than among the more educated, among Muslims than among Christians, Buddhists and Hindus, and among non-working women than those working before marriage (annex table D.3).

As noted earlier, since 1980 there has been a decline in the proportion of women who married or, more appropriately stated, were married off, below age 16 years (see table 29). Studies also indicate that the average age at marriage of females has been increasing throughout the country, reaching 21.1 years in 1990. These changes have been due to a combination of several factors. In the first instance, the Marriage Law enacted in 1974 set the minimum age at marriage at 16 years for girls and 19 years for boys. Second, since 1983, the government had encouraged the delay

of marriage until 20 years for females and 25 years for males. Third, over the past two decades, there have also been socio-cultural and economic changes which have influenced the way young persons perceive marriage. Increased access to education and the rising educational attainment of females have led to delay or postponement of their marriage. The nature of the marriage institution itself is undergoing significant change, from a traditional pattern of arranged marriages to a modern one characterized by self-selection of partners.

The trend towards a decrease in the proportion of early marriages and an increase in average age at first marriage is also reflected in the rising proportion of persons remaining unmarried or never married at younger or socially desirable marriageable ages. Data from the censuses indicate that between 1980 and 1990, the proportion of males and females reported as single or never married had increased at all ages between 15 and 49 years, and that this increase was more marked at ages 15-29 years, and among females than males at ages 15-19 years. Although the proportions unmarried are higher among males than females at all ages, in 1990, about 82 per cent of the females at ages 15-19 years and 36 per cent at ages 20-24 years were reported to be unmarried. The proportion remaining unmarried also decreases with increase in age, suggesting that young men and women now tend to refrain from early marriage but enter into marital union at a later stage.

The proportions never married are also higher in urban than rural areas and this differential is more marked at ages 20-24 years and above for males and at ages 15-19 years and above for females. In 1990, the proportion of never-married females at all age groups from 20 to 49 years in urban areas was twice or more than twice the corresponding proportion in rural areas (table 30).

(b) Reproductive behaviour

During the past three decades, Indonesia has witnessed significant changes not only in marriage patterns but also in the reproductive behaviour of Indonesian women. In particular,

Table 30. Percentage never married by age group, sex and residence: 1980 and 1990

Age group	Indonesia				Urban area				Rural area			
	Male		Female		Male		Female		Male		Female	
	1980	1990	1980	1990	1980	1990	1980	1990	1980	1990	1980	1990
10-14	99.1	99.3	99.1	99.7	99.4	99.4	99.6	99.8	99.0	99.2	98.0	99.6
15-19	96.3	97.6	70.0	81.8	97.7	98.5	82.0	90.9	95.8	97.0	65.6	76.5
20-24	59.5	71.7	22.2	35.7	74.2	82.6	36.8	53.4	53.5	64.7	17.2	25.3
25-29	19.7	29.0	7.7	11.2	32.6	42.1	13.7	19.0	15.3	22.0	5.8	7.3
30-34	6.1	9.4	3.4	4.4	11.1	14.2	6.5	7.3	4.5	6.9	2.5	3.1
35-39	2.6	4.6	1.9	2.7	4.8	6.4	3.5	4.5	2.0	3.8	1.5	1.9
40-44	1.6	3.4	1.4	2.0	2.2	4.4	2.3	3.3	1.4	3.0	1.2	1.6
45-49	1.2	2.9	1.0	1.4	2.5	3.6	1.9	2.3	0.8	2.6	1.1	1.1
50-54	1.0	2.7	1.3	1.3	1.5	3.2	1.5	1.9	0.8	2.6	1.2	1.0
55-59	1.0	2.6	1.0	1.1	1.6	2.9	1.8	1.6	0.8	2.4	0.8	0.9
60-64	0.9	2.4	1.4	1.2	2.0	2.7	2.1	1.6	0.7	2.4	1.3	1.0
65-69	1.0	2.9	1.3	1.3	1.9	3.5	1.1	1.9	0.9	2.7	1.3	1.1
70-74	1.2	2.9	1.2	1.3	2.0	4.1	0.9	2.6	0.9	3.3	1.3	1.7
75+	1.7	5.4	1.7	2.8	3.3	6.3	2.9	3.0	0.9	5.2	1.4	2.7
All ages	42.0	43.9	30.7	33.4	49.2	49.6	38.4	40.6	39.6	41.3	28.3	30.0

Sources: Central Bureau of Statistics, *Population of Indonesia: Results of the 1980 Population Census;* and *Results of the 1990 Population Census.*

the attitude of married couples in regard to the desired family size has undergone significant transition, as evidenced by declining trends in fertility rates. For instance, the total fertility rate declined rapidly from a high of 5.61 in 1971 to 2.85 in 1994. Available data indicate that the sharp decline in fertility occurred in all 27 provinces and that in some provinces, including a few outer island provinces, fertility has been reduced to replacement level.

Age-specific fertility rates also indicate that there has been a gradual decline in the fertility of women in younger age groups (15-19 and 20-24 years), reflecting the effects of both delays in marriage and the smaller number of childbirths among women in these age groups. These data also show that over the years there has been a shift in the peak fertility age group from 20-24 years to the next higher age group, 25-29 years (table 31), reflecting delayed age at first childbirth.

The decline in fertility that had occurred in the country over the years has largely been due to the success of the government's intensive family planning programme in increasing the knowledge about as well as access to and use of contraceptives by couples at reproductive ages. According to the 1994 Demographic and Health Survey, 95.7 per cent of ever-married women and 96.3 per cent of currently married women aged 15-49 years reported knowing at least one family planning method, and virtually all of them knew about at least one modern method. Data from various surveys conducted over the years also show that knowledge of most modern contraceptive methods among currently married women had increased since 1987, and that this increase in knowledge has been more marked in respect of Norplant, male sterilization and female sterilization (figure 8).

The proportion of currently married women aged 15-49 years using contraception has also been increasing in recent years and, according to the 1994 Survey, about 55 per cent of currently married women were using contraception, with 52 per cent using modern methods and 3 per cent traditional methods. The Survey also showed that pills, injection and IUD were the most commonly used methods, together accounting for 78 per cent of current contraceptive use. While modern methods were popular among women of all ages, contraceptive prevalence was reported to be higher among women in mid-childbearing ages (25-39 years) than among young and older women (table 32).

Table 31. Age-specific fertility and total fertility rates: 1971-1994

Age groups	Age-specific fertility rates						
	1971 census (1967-1970)	1980 census (1976-1979)	1987 National Indonesia Contraceptive Prevalence Survey (1984-1987)	1990 census (1986-1989)	1994 Demographic and Health Survey (1991-1994)		
					Total	Urban	Rural
15-19	155	116	78	71	61	34	78
20-24	286	248	188	178	147	108	170
25-29	273	232	172	172	150	141	155
30-34	211	177	126	128	109	105	110
35-39	124	104	75	73	68	57	73
40-44	55	46	29	31	31	16	38
45-49	17	13	10	9	4	1	5
Total fertility rate	5.61	4.68	3.39	3.31	2.85	2.31	3.15

Source: Central Bureau of Statistics and others, *Indonesia Demographic and Health Survey, 1994.*

Figure 8. Percentage of currently married women who know specific modern contraceptive methods: 1987, 1991 and 1994

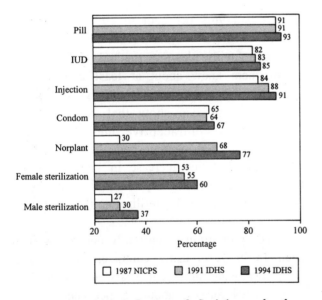

Source: Central Bureau of Statistics and others, *Indonesia Demographic and Health Survey, 1994.*

IDHS: Indonesia Demographic and Health Survey.
NICPS: National Indonesia Contraceptive Prevalence Survey.

As is to be expected, a higher proportion of women in urban than in rural areas uses family planning methods. The 1994 Demographic and Health Survey reported that the proportion of currently married women using a contraceptive method was 60.2 per cent in urban areas and 52.5 per cent in rural areas. The Survey also showed that contraceptive use increased with the respondent's level of education, from 40 per cent of currently married women with no education to 63 per cent among those with secondary or higher educational attainment. Contraceptive use also increased with the number of living children a woman had; while only 9.0 per cent of women with no children were currently using a method, this proportion was as high as 65.4 per cent among women with three children. The Survey also revealed major differentials in contraceptive use between regions, being highest (58.4 per cent) in Java-Bali and lowest (45.7) in Outer Java Bali II (see annex table D.4 and figure 9).

According to the 1994 Survey, 48 per cent of currently married women aged 15-49 years reported that they wanted no more children, while another 4.0 per cent had been sterilized and another 4.0 per cent were not sure whether they wanted another child. Of the 4.3 per cent who indicated they wanted to have additional children, 14 per cent wanted the child within two years, 25 per cent after two years and 4 per cent were not sure when they wanted to have the additional children (see figure 10).

The 1994 Survey also reported that more than half of the married women with two living children wanted no more children or had been

42

Table 32. Percentage distribution of currently married women currently using a contraceptive method, according to age: 1994

Age group	Any method	Any modern method	Any traditional method	Not currently using contraception	Total
15-19	36.4	35.6	0.8	63.6	100.0
20-24	55.5	54.0	1.5	44.5	100.0
25-29	59.6	57.8	1.8	40.4	100.0
30-34	61.0	57.5	3.4	39.0	100.0
35-39	59.7	56.2	3.5	40.3	100.0
40-44	53.4	49.5	3.9	46.6	100.0
45-49	32.9	30.1	2.8	67.1	100.0
All ages	54.7	52.1	2.7	45.3	100.0

Source: Central Bureau of Statistics and others, *Indonesia Demographic and Health Survey, 1994.*

Figure 9. Percentage of currently married women aged 15-49 years currently using a contraceptive method, by background characteristics: 1994

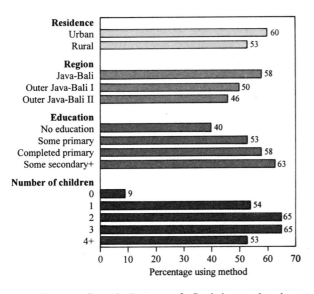

Source: Central Bureau of Statistics and others, *Indonesia Demographic and Health Survey, 1994.*

Figure 10. Fertility preference of currently married women aged 15-49 years

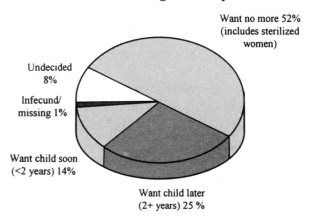

Source: Central Bureau of Statistics and others, *Indonesia Demographic and Health Survey, 1994.*

sterilized; about 71 per cent of women with three living children either wanted no more children or had been sterilized; and another about 15 per cent wanted to delay the birth for at least two years (table 33).

The 1994 Survey also revealed that the desire to stop childbearing was significantly higher in urban areas (56.1 per cent) than in rural areas (49.7 per cent), in the Java-Bali region (53.3 per cent) compared with Outer-Java Bali I (49.0 per cent) and Outer Java Bali II (47.3 per cent). A rather strange finding of

the Survey was that this desire to stop childbearing was higher among women with no education (59.6 per cent) than among women with secondary education (45.8 per cent). The Survey showed that the proportion of currently married women desiring no more children decreased with increasing educational attainment (annex table D.5).

(c) Marital disruption

Persons who are widowed or divorced belong to that segment of the population living in a state of marital disruption. These events which occur among married persons have the effect of reducing the proportion of currently married persons. In Indonesia, as in most other countries, census data on the marital status of the population constitute an important

Table 33. Percentage distribution of currently married women by desire for more children, according to number of living children: 1994

Desire for children	Number of living children[a]							Total
	0	1	2	3	4	5	6+	
Have another soon[b]	77.6	23.2	10.9	5.8	3.1	1.9	0.9	14.4
Have another later[c]	11.5	59.8	26.8	14.6	8.3	4.2	2.2	24.8
Have another, undecided when	4.2	6.0	4.6	2.7	2.2	1.3	1.2	3.7
Undecided	1.5	2.6	5.8	5.2	3.8	4.2	5.4	4.3
Want no more	2.9	7.4	49.7	65.3	73.0	78.1	79.7	47.8
Sterilized	0.1	0.3	1.7	5.7	8.4	7.7	6.8	3.7
Declared in found	2.2	0.9	0.5	0.8	1.1	2.3	3.7	1.3
Missing	–	–	0.1	–	0.2	0.2	0.1	0.1
Total	100.0	100.0	100.0	100.0	100.0	100.0	100.0	100.0

Source: Central Bureau of Statistics and others, *Indonesia Demographic and Health Survey, 1994.*

[a] Including current preqnancy.
[b] Want next birth within two years.
[c] Want to delay next birth for two or more years.

source for analysing the trends and patterns of marital disruption.

The age-sex-specific proportions of widowed persons (calculated as a percentage of ever-married persons) in 1980 and 1990 are given in table 34.

It is evident from table 34 that the incidence of widowhood among ever-married males and females is relatively low at young ages, except at ages 10-14 years, and that starting from the 15-19 age group these proportions increase with advancing age, reflecting the higher mortality risks at older ages. It will also be noted that the proportions widowed are higher among females than males in practically all age groups. This gender disparity also increases with age; in 1990, for instance, the difference in the proportion widowed between males and

Table 34. Percentage widowed among ever-married males and females by age group: censuses of 1980 and 1990

Age group	1980		1990					
	Indonesia		Indonesia		Urban		Rural	
	Male	Female	Male	Female	Male	Female	Male	Female
10-14	2.7	3.6	4.5	4.6	5.0	6.3	4.4	4.3
15-19	1.5	1.0	1.5	0.4	1.7	0.5	1.6	0.4
20-24	0.6	0.9	0.5	0.6	0.4	0.6	0.5	0.6
25-29	0.4	1.6	0.4	1.0	0.3	0.9	0.4	1.1
30-34	0.6	3.2	0.6	2.1	0.4	1.9	0.6	2.2
35-39	0.9	5.4	0.8	4.0	0.6	3.7	0.8	4.2
40-44	1.4	11.4	1.4	8.8	1.1	8.1	1.6	9.0
45-49	2.2	15.5	2.0	14.0	1.6	13.8	2.2	14.0
50-54	3.5	28.9	3.5	24.0	3.0	24.2	3.7	24.0
55-59	4.4	34.8	3.3	31.4	4.4	33.3	4.9	30.8
60-64	7.0	53.4	7.6	47.2	7.4	47.1	7.6	47.2
65-69	10.2	58.2	9.6	55.0	9.8	55.9	9.5	54.6
70-74	14.3	71.2	14.4	70.5	14.5	70.6	14.3	70.4
75+	23.0	78.8	23.6	78.4	24.3	79.4	23.4	78.1
All ages	2.8	15.1	2.9	14.0	2.4	13.3	3.1	14.0

Source: Central Bureau of Statistics, population censuses of 1980 and 1990.

44

females increased from 7.4 percentage points at ages 40-44 years to 50.1 percentage points at ages 70-74 years. There is hardly any significant difference in the age-sex-specific proportions widowed between urban and rural areas.

The substantially higher incidence of widowhood among females compared with males is attributed to several factors. First, Indonesia women generally marry men who are their senior in age and the chances are that husbands will die before their wives. Second, the higher mortality and low life expectancy for males result in a situation in which more men than women become widowed, particularly at older ages. Third, several Indonesian men tend to have more than one spouse, and the death of the man would result in two or more women becoming widowed. Fourth, widowed men have better chances of remarriage than their female counterparts and thus end their state of marital disruption.

Several studies have shown that over the years there has been a gradual decline in divorce rates in Indonesia. Data from the censuses also show that between 1980 and 1990, the overall proportions divorced among the ever married declined from 2.0 to 1.8 per cent for males and from 5.9 to 4.6 per cent for females. This decline has generally been attributed to the increase in age at first marriage and in free choice of spouses or love marriages.

The age-sex-specific divorce rates among ever-married persons aged 10 years and over given in table 35 show that the incidence of divorce or marital dissolution is relatively higher among very young persons, 10-19 years old, compared with those at older ages. This would suggest that early marriages often lead to early family dissolution since such marriages are arranged marriages between boys and girls who are perfect strangers and may not be attracted to each other. A 1979 study (Ishmael: 1979) reported that many child marriages in Indramayu soon end in divorce, and that it was not unusual to see young boys and girls sitting on the long benches in front of the local religious court waiting to have their marriages annulled. A 1997 study (Savitridina: 1997) also found that in Java one third of all women who married early experienced dissolution of their first marriage, and that women who married early were three times more likely to find their first marriage dissolved than women who married later.

Table 35. Percentage divorced among ever-married males and females by age group: censuses of 1980 and 1990

Age group	1980 Indonesia		1990 Indonesia		1990 Urban		1990 Rural	
	Male	Female	Male	Female	Male	Female	Male	Female
10-14	3.2	12.8	5.9	8.1	5.8	5.4	6.0	8.6
15-19	7.4	8.0	6.4	6.0	3.2	4.9	7.2	6.2
20-24	4.6	6.2	3.5	4.8	2.0	4.2	3.9	5.0
25-29	2.7	5.3	2.3	4.2	1.5	4.0	2.5	4.3
30-34	1.8	5.2	1.7	4.2	1.4	4.2	1.9	4.1
35-39	1.6	4.8	1.4	4.2	1.3	4.4	1.4	4.1
40-44	1.5	5.9	1.4	4.7	1.4	4.7	1.4	4.6
45-49	1.4	5.7	1.3	4.9	1.3	5.0	1.4	4.8
50-54	1.5	6.6	1.5	5.4	1.4	5.6	1.5	5.3
55-59	1.3	6.5	1.0	5.2	1.4	5.2	1.4	5.2
60-64	1.6	6.6	1.6	5.3	1.5	5.0	1.6	5.4
65-69	1.9	6.3	1.6	4.9	1.4	4.7	1.6	5.0
70-74	2.1	5.6	1.8	4.6	1.5	4.3	1.9	4.7
75+	2.2	4.2	2.4	3.4	2.0	3.0	2.5	3.5
All ages	2.0	5.9	1.8	4.6	1.5	4.5	1.9	4.6

Source: Central Bureau of Statistics, population censuses of 1980 and 1990.

It is also evident from table 35 that divorce rates are higher among ever-married females than males at practically all ages in both urban and rural areas, and that this gender disparity is more pronounced at ages 30 years and above than at younger ages. Further, although the overall incidence of divorce among males and females is about the same in urban as in rural areas, at the younger age groups, 10-24 years, the divorce rates are significantly higher in rural than in urban areas for both males and females. The 1997 study mentioned earlier also reported that 31 per cent of women living in rural Java were no longer in their first marriage; the corresponding proportions for women living in big cities and towns were 20 and 23 per cent. The study also reported that the tendency towards marital dissolution increased from the lowest level in cities to the highest level in rural areas, irrespective of whether women married early or late.

Several studies have reported that the divorce rate is inversely related to social status. Among the Javanese ordinary villagers (*abangan*), for instance, divorce is not considered morally wrong, as it is seen as the best solution to irreconcilable conflicts between husband and wife. Since she is not dependent on her husband for economic support, an *abangan* wife is fully prepared to continue to take care of herself after divorce. On the other hand, women from upper-income or elite families tend to try to avoid divorce as they are economically dependent on their husbands. Among the Sudanese, the more frequently a woman marries and divorces, the greater her social prestige, because she has to be attractive to get married frequently.

3. Domestic violence

In Indonesia, as in many other countries, accurate and comprehensive data on domestic violence are not available. By and large, cases of domestic violence are not reported as they are amicably settled within the household, and police records do not classify the few reported cases as domestic violence. While domestic violence against women remains a "hidden problem", it is generally accepted that wife abuse/battering is a fairly serious problem in the country.

It is also generally agreed that violence against women, particularly sexual violence, is a daily phenomenon throughout the country. In 1994 alone, there were more than 3,000 recorded cases of rape, and in more than 25 per cent of these cases the victims were girls aged 15-17 years. It is generally conceded that there is gross under-reporting of cases of sexual violence against women. Female victims seldom report the offence committed against them for fear of being shamed or stigmatized, and many of them do not know to whom and where they should report. Contrary to public perception, rape is not always committed by strangers; in about 75 per cent of the reported cases, the alleged offenders were known persons such as friend, neighbour, work colleague, teacher etc.

Data from Police Headquarters show that the vast majority of the victims in reported cases of violence over the three-year period 1992-1994 were women; of the 3,769 cases of reported violence in 1994, in as many as 3,000 cases, or about 80 per cent, women were the victims (table 36).

Table 36. Reported cases of violence by sex of victim: 1992-1994

Year	Both sexes		Male		Female	
	Number of cases	Percentage	Number of cases	Percentage	Number of cases	Percentage
1992	2 825	100.0	503	17.8	2 322	82.2
1993	4 098	100.0	895	21.8	3 203	78.2
1994	3 769	100.0	769	20.4	3 000	79.6

Source: Police Headquarters.

E. WOMEN IN ECONOMIC LIFE

1. Background

The role of women in economic life can be viewed in terms of their participation in the labour force, or more specifically in their employment. Traditionally, Indonesian women had played an important part in economic activities, in particular by involving themselves in family or household enterprises such as farming, livestock and poultry raising, cottage industries etc. The participation of women in economic production has been in addition to their day-to-day responsibility for domestic chores such as housekeeping, fetching water for domestic use, cooking meals for family members and caring for and rearing children. In recent decades, however, with increasing educational attainment and expanding employment opportunities, women have begun to engage in work outside the home in both the formal and informal sectors.

In recognition of the increasing entry of women into the formal labour market, the government has enacted several special laws and regulations to provide legal safeguards and stipulations in regard to the employment and working conditions of women. For example, employers are debarred from terminating the services of a female employee for reasons of marriage, pregnancy or childbirth. On the other hand, women workers are entitled to full pay during the three months' maternity leave as well as time off during work to nurse their infants. Further, employers must not discriminate between male and female workers in determining the rates of remuneration for work of equal value.

The special labour regulations also require employers to provide separate toilets for men and women in workplaces. An establishment employing a large number of females must provide several well-lit and spacious rest rooms and toilets for their use. Government regulations also do not permit the employment of women during night hours or to work underground (mines), or perform duties which might be against moral ethics or endanger their health.

Although originally intended to ensure equal employment opportunities and an appropriate working environment for women, the special labour laws and regulations appear to have some adverse effects on women's employment. For instance, there is an increasing tendency not to assign important and responsible tasks to female employees because of possible long absence on maternity leave. Several establishments also observe an unwritten policy of hiring only single female workers owing to the high rate of absenteeism among married women workers. The prohibition of women working during night hours has resulted in some factories not hiring women in large numbers as they cannot be assigned to night shifts.

Nevertheless, several measures have been initiated by the Indonesian Government and non-governmental organizations to educate women workers regarding their legally guaranteed rights and entitlements. Attempts are also being made to enhance the participation of women in economic activities by, among other things, improving their skills and capabilities, thereby increasing their chances for employment in various fields; promoting cooperative projects managed by women; and providing practical guidance and training to enable small businesswomen to improve their entrepreneurial spirit and capability.

2. Database

Data on economic activity collected by the Central Bureau of Statistics reflect the labour-force concept which refers to a group of persons who are working in gainful employment, or are wanting or looking for such work during a specified period preceding the inquiry. The 1990 Indonesian census, for instance, defined the labour force as including all persons aged 10 years and over who, during the one week prior to the time of enumeration: (a) were not jobless, in the sense that they either worked or temporarily did not work owing to slack time in their work, such as waiting for harvest, being on leave, and the like; or (b) were jobless but actively looking for work. Thus, persons aged 10 years and over who, during the reference week, did nothing other than attending school, housekeeping, or "other", were deemed to be not in the labour force.

A comparative analysis of trends in labour-force participation over time is, however, rendered somewhat difficult owing to differences in the reference or time period and definition of the "employed" adopted in the censuses. The time reference used for determining activity status was a six-month period prior to the date of enumeration, but only a week prior to the enumeration date at the 1971 and subsequent censuses. The 1961 census defined the "employed" as those "carrying out a job for pay", including persons who were not working on the enumeration date but had worked for at least two months during the preceding six months. In the 1971 census, the "employed" included persons who worked for pay or profit for at least two days in the one-week period prior to the enumeration date. Persons who worked less than two days or who did not work but had permanent jobs, or who did not work because of illness, being on leave or on strike, were also counted as being employed. At the 1980 and 1990 censuses, the criterion adopted for classifying a person as working was at least one hour of work in the previous week.

For purposes of this profile, the analysis of shifts in patterns of labour-force participation is based on the data from the 1980 and 1990 population censuses which have used identical reference periods and definitions of employed or working persons.

3. Labour-force participation

Although females outnumber males in working ages 10 years and over, female participation in the labour force was substantially lower than that of males in 1980 as well as in 1990. In 1990, for instance, females constituted

about 51 per cent of all persons aged 10 years and over but accounted for only 36 per cent of the total economically active population or labour force. In other words, about 64 per cent of females aged 10 years and over were economically inactive, the corresponding proportion among males being about 36 per cent. Consequently, the overall labour-force participation rate, or the economically active as a proportion of persons aged 10 years and over, for females (38.7 per cent) was almost half the rate of 71.1 per cent for males in 1990 (annex table E.1 and table 37).

It is also evident from annex table E.1 and table 37 that between 1980 and 1990 there was a substantial increase in the country's labour force or economically active population, and that this increase was more marked in the case of females than males. While the male labour force increased by 35.4 per cent, from 35.0 million in 1980 to 47.4 million in 1990, the female labour force increased by 55.0 per cent, from 17.1 million to 26.5 million, during the same period. Consequently, the annual rate of growth of the labour force averaged 5.5 per cent for females and 3.6 per cent for males between 1980 and 1990.

The faster growth of the female labour force between 1980 and 1990 is attributed to several factors. First, there was improved enumeration of women's economic activities in the 1990 census compared with the 1980 census, and the recorded rise in female labour-force participation partially reflects this statistical artefact. But more importantly, the increase reflects a significant genuine increase in female

Table 37. Labour-force participation of persons aged 10 years and over by sex: 1980 and 1990

Activity status	1980			1990		
	Both sexes	Male	Female	Both sexes	Male	Female
Percentage of all persons 10 years and over	100.0	49.2	50.8	100.0	49.6	50.6
Percentage of economically active persons	100.0	67.2	32.8	100.0	64.1	35.9
Percentage of not economically active persons	100.0	32.8	67.2	100.0	35.6	64.1
Labour-force participation rate[a]	49.6	68.1	32.2	54.7	71.1	38.7

Source: Annex table E.1.

[a] Economically active persons as a proportion of persons aged 10 years and over.

48

labour-force participation resulting from women's increased educational attainment, decreasing domestic responsibilities and rapidly expanding employment opportunities in the formal as well as informal sectors of the economy.

In terms of time utilization, women have the option of either staying at home to perform household chores or entering the labour market to earn income. Data from the 1980 and 1990 censuses show that an ever larger number of women have chosen the second alternative. In 1980, the number of women staying at home and attending to housekeeping (21.8 million) was substantially larger than their number in the labour force (17.1 million). But by 1990, this situation was reversed when the number of economically active females (26.5 million) was higher than the 24.8 million reported as engaged in housekeeping (annex table E.1). In other words, the ratio of women engaged in house-keeping to economically active declined from 1.250 in 1980 to 0.937 in 1990. This change provides some indication that the additional worker hypothesis may be true in Indonesia. Women respond to the need for additional household income by entering the labour market.

Further, the success of the family planning programme in reducing the average number of children per woman and the consequent lessening of women's burden for child care has resulted in more time being available to women to engage in productive activities. The implementation of the higher legal minimum age at marriage has tended to increase women's demand for employment, while their improved educational attainment has led to an increase in their demand for more and better jobs.

It must, however, be emphasized that the increasing participation of women in the labour force was also facilitated by growing demand for labour or expanding employment opportunities. The various deregulation measures adopted by the government during the 1980s worked towards opening more job opportunities for males and females in the secondary (manufacturing, utilities and construction) and in the tertiary (trade, transport, finance, service and "other") sectors. Thus, the situation of the female workforce in Indonesia was better than in many other developing countries, where the labour-force participation rates, particularly of females, decreased significantly during the period of structural adjustment in the 1980s.

Data from the 1980 and 1990 censuses also show that the overall labour-force participation rates for both males and females are significantly higher in rural than in urban areas. In 1990, for example, the participation rate for urban males (64.0 per cent) was 10.4 percentage points lower than that for rural males (74.4 per cent). Similarly, the rate for urban females (31.6 per cent) was 10.6 percentage points lower than the 42.2 per cent reported for rural females (table 38).

The urban-rural differential in the labour-force participation rate is due to two important factors. The first is the larger concentration of middle- and upper-class families in urban than in rural areas. A substantially higher proportion of boys and girls from rich or higher-income families continue with their schooling, while poverty compels children from low-income families to drop out of school and join the labour force in order to supplement the meagre

Table 38. Labour-force participation rates by residence and sex: 1980 and 1990

(Percentage)

Sex	1980			1990		
	Indonesia	Urban	Rural	Indonesia	Urban	Rural
Both sexes	49.9	41.4	52.6	54.7	47.6	58.1
Male	68.1	58.9	70.9	71.1	64.0	74.4
Female	32.2	24.1	34.9	38.7	31.6	42.2

Source: Central Bureau of Statistics, population censuses of 1980 and 1990.

household income. The second factor is that opportunities for self-employment as well as for unpaid work in family or household enterprises are much higher in rural than in urban areas.

As noted earlier, the overall percentage increase in the labour force or economically active persons between 1980 and 1990 was substantially higher among females (55.0 per cent) compared with males (34.4 per cent). The higher increase in the female than the male labour force occurred at all age groups but was especially large among young adult women; 50.3 per cent of the total increase in the female labour force was contributed by increases among women aged 20-34 years and another approximately 10 per cent by those aged 35-39 years (annex table E.2).

The age-specific labour-force participation rates given in table 39 indicate that for the country as a whole there was an increase in these rates at all ages 15 years and over between 1980 and 1990, and that these increases were more pronounced for females than males. At ages 10-14, however, the participation rate for both males and females had declined during this period owing to increased school enrolment ratios. It is also evident from table 39 that participation rates for females are substantially

lower than the corresponding male rates at all age groups in both urban and rural areas. Generally, the participation rates for rural females were also significantly higher than those of urban females.

It will also be noted from table 39 that labour-force participation rates for both males and females increase with advancing age until the peak ages of participation, and then decrease gradually. The participation rates rise precipitously between ages 10-14 and 15-19 years, reaching a peak at ages 35-39 years for males and 45-49 years for females. In 1990, the peak rate was 98.0 per cent for males and 53.9 for females, a difference of 44.1 percentage points. The 1990 data also show that while the peak age of participation is the same (35-39 years) for males in urban as well as in rural areas, the female rate reaches a peak at ages 40-44 years in urban areas and at 45-49 years in rural areas (see also figure 11).

Labour-force participation rates also vary according to the level of educational attainment for both males and females in rural as well as in urban areas. Participation rates for women with no schooling were higher than those for women with some primary education or who had completed primary or lower secondary

Table 39. Labour-force participation rates by age group, residence and sex: 1980 and 1990

(Percentage)

Age group	1980 Indonesia		1990 Indonesia		1990 Urban		1990 Rural	
	Male	Female	Male	Female	Male	Female	Male	Female
10-14	12.7	9.4	11.9	8.8	4.3	5.0	15.0	10.5
15-19	47.4	31.1	47.6	33.6	28.6	27.4	57.5	37.2
20-24	79.2	34.0	80.0	43.5	68.6	41.0	87.3	44.9
25-29	92.1	35.9	94.3	45.7	90.5	39.8	96.4	48.6
30-34	94.8	39.2	97.6	48.4	96.7	39.1	98.0	52.9
35-39	95.3	42.4	98.0	51.4	97.4	40.5	98.3	56.2
40-44	94.7	45.7	97.7	53.4	97.1	41.2	98.0	58.3
45-49	93.7	46.5	96.8	53.9	95.3	40.9	97.5	58.9
50-54	89.7	44.0	94.2	51.6	90.1	39.2	95.8	56.4
55-59	84.2	40.4	89.3	48.1	78.3	34.2	93.4	53.5
60-64	76.3	32.7	80.5	40.3	62.4	28.0	86.9	44.7
65+	53.1	18.8	59.3	23.5	42.6	16.4	64.8	26.1
All ages 10+	67.2	32.8	71.1	38.8	64.0	31.6	74.4	42.2

Source: Central Bureau of Statistics, population censuses of 1980 and 1990.

Figure 11. Age-sex specific labour-force participation rates by residence: 1990

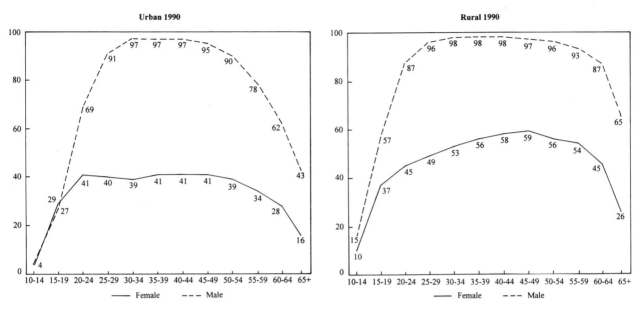

Source: Central Bureau of Statistics, 1990 population census.

education, but lower than those for women with upper secondary or higher levels of educational attainment. For the country as a whole, the peak participation rates for both males and females were reported in respect of those who had completed university education. Between 1980 and 1990, there were significant increases in the participation rates of women with various levels of educational attainment in rural and urban areas. Nevertheless, the male participation rates were higher than the corresponding rates for females at all levels of educational attainment in urban as well as rural areas (annex table E.3).

The marital status pattern of the economically active males and females more or less conforms to the pattern of the total population. According to the 1990 census data, almost all economically active males and females aged 10-14 years in rural as well as urban areas were unmarried. The proportion unmarried decreases with increasing age for both the sexes. In the case of the economically active females, while the proportion widowed with advancing age reaches a peak of about 65 per cent in urban and rural areas, the proportion married increases with age to reach a peak at ages 35-39 and thereafter declines gradually (annex table E.4).

4. Employed labour force

As noted earlier, the economically active population or labour force has been defined as including the working or employed persons as well as those looking for work or employment. According to the 1990 census, a person was deemed to be working or employed if, during the week prior to the enumeration, he/she:

(a) Worked or assisted in a certain job for at least one continuous hour to earn income; or

(b) Did not work at all or worked for less than one hour but happened to be a permanent worker or government employee who was on leave, on strike or sick, or had to stop working as a result of irregularities such as machinery problems; or happened to be farmers in their slack time waiting for harvest or rainfall; or professionals who had to wait for their customers.

The 1990 census also defined those looking for work as persons who, during the week prior to the enumeration, were employed but for some reason were still looking for work; were laid off and had a promise of re-employment but were actively looking for work; or were unemployed and actively looking for work.

51

According to the data from the 1980 and 1990 censuses, the vast majority of males as well as females reckoned to be economically active or in the current labour force were working or employed in terms of the criteria mentioned in the preceding paragraph, but in both years this proportion was slightly higher for males than for females. In 1990, for instance, 97.2 per cent of the economically active males were reported to be working or employed, the corresponding proportion for females being 96.1 per cent (table 40).

(a) Industrial attachment

The numerical distribution of the employed persons by major industrial sector in 1980 and 1990 is shown in annex table E.5, while the percentage distribution is given in table 41. It will be noted that in 1980, as well as in 1990, the highest proportion of employed males and females was engaged in the major industrial group of agriculture, forestry, hunting and fishing, which is the lowest productivity sector. It will also be noted from annex table E.5 that there have been substantial increases in the number of workers in the agriculture and allied industrial sector, but this growth has been more pronounced for female than for males, leading to a feminization of the agricultural workforce. Although, compared with females, the number of males in the agricultural labour force was almost twice as large in 1980 and in 1990, the increase during the 1980s in the female agricultural labour force (3.7 million) was almost as large as that for males (4.0 million). Consequently, the percentage increase in the female

Table 40. Percentage distribution of economically active persons aged 10 years and over by activity status and sex: 1980 and 1990

Activity status	1980			1990		
	Both sexes	Male	Female	Both sexes	Male	Female
Working	98.2	98.5	97.6	96.8	97.2	96.1
Looking for work	1.8	1.5	2.4	3.2	2.8	3.9
Total	100.0	100.0	100.0	100.0	100.0	100.0

Source: Central Bureau of Statistics, population censuses of 1980 and 1990.

Table 41. Percentage distribution of employed persons aged 10 years and over by major industrial sector and sex: 1980 and 1990

Major industrial sector	1980		1990	
	Male	Female	Male	Female
Agriculture, forestry, hunting and fishing	55.9	52.5	50.5	48.9
Mining and quarrying	0.9	0.4	1.3	0.5
Manufacturing industry	7.3	11.0	9.8	14.4
Electricity, gas and water	0.2	0.1	0.3	–
Construction	4.4	0.3	6.2	0.3
Wholesale and retail trade, restaurants and hotels	10.0	18.8	11.8	19.9
Transport, storage and communications	4.2	0.1	5.6	0.2
Finance, insurance, real estate and business services	0.6	0.2	1.1	0.6
Social and personal services	15.3	14.7	12.7	13.7
Others	0.1	0.1	–	0.1
Industry not stated	1.1	1.8	0.6	1.4
All industrial sectors	100.0	100.0	100.0	100.0

Source: Central Bureau of Statistics, population censuses of 1980 and 1990.

A dash (–) indicates that the number is negligible.

agricultural labour force (42.1 per cent) was more than twice that for males (20.8 per cent).

Despite the substantial increases in the number of male and female agricultural workers between 1980 and 1990, their relative share in the total number of workers had declined significantly during this period, from 55.9 to 50.5 per cent among males and from 52.5 to 48.9 per cent among females. While these declining proportions are in conformity with the decreasing contribution of the agricultural sector to total GDP, it would appear that the sectoral shift required by the modernization process has been slower for female than for male workers.

Nevertheless, with the overall increase in the proportion of woman in the total labour force, there have been marked increases in women's employment in the non-agricultural sectors, especially manufacturing and trade, during the 1980s. The number of female workers in the manufacturing sector almost doubled, from 1.84 million in 1980 to 3.66 million in 1990, compared with an increase from 2.52 million to 4.52 million, or by 79 per cent, in the number of male workers during the same period. Consequently, the relative share of workers in the manufacturing sector rose from 11.0 to 14.4 per cent for females and from 7.3 to 9.8 per cent for males (annex table E.5 and table 41). Available data also indicate that within the manufacturing sector, female workers are largely concentrated in textiles, electronics, food processing, tobacco processing and cigarette factories, while males are employed in larger numbers in chemicals, paper products and metal industries.

There has also been a rather large increase in the number of women employed in the trade sector, by about 1.94 million from 3.14 million in 1980 to 5.08 million in 1990. In absolute terms, this increase was almost equal to the corresponding increase in male workers from 3.47 million to 5.46 million, or by 1.99 million, during the same period. The proportionate share of workers engaged in the trade sector increased from 18.8 to 19.9 per cent for females, and from 10.0 to 11.8 per cent for males (annex table E.5 and table 41).

The substantial shift towards the trade sector has become a significant issue for the country because this sector also happens to be a low productivity sector. Trade is also an important area of informal sector activity for women. Available data indicate that a higher proportion among women (27 per cent) than men (16 per cent) are concentrated in trade. According to the 1990 census, 34 per cent of female employment in the urban areas was in the trade sector, this proportion for males being considerably lower, at 22 per cent. Most women workers in trade operate as market traders, sidewalk traders and stall-keepers, while mobile trading is almost exclusively male-dominated. The majority of female-dominated activities in trade are related to women's domestic roles, particularly the production and sale of food, and are characterized by long working hours but low earnings. Women go into trading mainly because it does not require much skill or capital to get started, and in general they have few other options.

Although the number of women workers in the social and personal service sector had increased substantially, from 2.46 million in 1980 to 3.50 million in 1990, the proportion of women workers employed in this sector decreased from 14.7 to 13.7 per cent during this period. Women are also making inroads into the highly productive finance sector; the number of women workers in this sector increased more than fourfold, from 35,854 in 1980 to 156,876 in 1990. But the numbers involved are not large enough to have a meaningful impact structurally.

(b) Occupational structure

Occupations, or the kinds of work in which the employed persons spend most of their time during a specified time period, are structurally clustered into groupings which reflect a certain hierarchy in employment. This type of relationship is to some extent denoted by the International Standard Classification of Occupations adopted by most countries. For example, professionals and managers have a hierarchical status higher than that of clerical and production workers. But the professional category itself comprises occupations with varying social and hierarchical status. It is also not possible to establish a strict hierarchical relationship in regard to sales, service and production workers. Nevertheless, the occupational profile of employed persons provides a useful basis for ascertaining the extent to which women, vis-à-vis men, are employed in the type of occupation that would help enhance their welfare and social status.

The numerical distribution of employed persons by broad occupational category is given in annex table E.6, and their percentage distribution in table 42.

It will be noted from annex table E.6 and table 42 that the occupational structure of the employed persons more or less conforms to their pattern of industrial or sectoral attachment. The majority of male as well as female workers are engaged in agricultural and allied occupations, and although their numbers in this category increased between 1980 and 1990, there was a decline in their relative shares. In 1990, about 49 per cent of employed females and 50.4 per cent of employed males were reported to be agricultural and related workers.

The number of females engaged as professional, technical and related workers more than doubled, from 541,881 in 1980 to 1,129,093 in 1990, while their relative share in the total

number of women rose from 3.2 to 4.4 per cent during the same period. The remarkable increase in the number of women employed in professional and technical occupations has largely been due to an increase in the number engaged in the lower levels of this occupational category as teachers, nurses, paramedical personnel etc.

There has also been a substantial increase in the number of females engaged as sales workers and as production workers. Available data also indicate that the majority of women workers in these two occupational categories are employed in low-paid, low-status jobs. For instance, a 1991 World Bank study of enterprises in export-oriented manufacturing found that women were over-represented among the unskilled, slightly under-represented among skilled workers, and heavily under-represented among supervisors and technicians. An important reason for women being employed in low-status and low-paying jobs is that they lack the skills and educational qualifications to perform better jobs.

(c) Employment status

According to the international classification system, employed persons are disaggregated in terms of their employment status into four categories: employer, employee, self-employed or own-account worker, and unpaid family worker. According to the definitions adopted in the 1990 population census of Indonesia:

Table 42. Percentage distribution of employed persons aged 10 years and over by broad occupational category and sex: 1980 and 1990

Major industrial sector	1980		1990	
	Male	Female	Male	Female
Professional, technical and related workers	2.9	3.2	3.3	4.4
Administrative and managerial workers	0.1	0.1	0.3	0.1
Clerical and related workers	4.8	1.5	6.0	3.0
Sales workers	10.1	18.7	11.5	19.2
Service workers	3.1	7.8	2.7	6.8
Agricultural, animal husbandry and forestry workers, fishermen and hunters	55.7	52.4	50.4	48.9
Production and related workers, transport equipment operators, and labourers	21.1	14.3	25.3	16.3
Others	1.0	0.2	0.1	0.1
Occupation not stated	1.2	1.8	0.3	1.1
All occupations	100.0	100.0	100.0	100.0

Source: Central Bureau of Statistics, population censuses of 1980 and 1990.

- Employers are those in business who are assisted by permanent workers and who bear the entire business risks, as for example, a shop owner who employs one or more permanent workers, or a shoe-factory owner who employs permanent workers

- Employees are those who work for other people or an institution/agency/enterprise and who receive remuneration in cash or in kind, as for example, government officials, employees of government/private enterprises, hotel employees, or domestic servants

- The self-employed are those who either work on their own, such as tricycle drivers or taxi drivers, who bear the entire risk of their job/business; or work as labourers operating in market places, railway stations or similar places who have no particular employers

- Unpaid family workers are those who work for other people or other household economic enterprises without any form of payment, as, for example, children who assist in their family shops as shop attendants and wives who help their husbands on the family farm

The work relationship between employer and employee is usually formal and hence employers and paid employees are considered to be working in the formal sector, while self-employed and unpaid family workers are considered to be engaged in the informal sector. The numerical distribution of employed persons aged 10 years and over by employment status and sex in 1980 and 1990 is given in annex table E.7, and the percentage distribution in table 43.

A very high proportion of the Indonesian labour force is in the informal sector, engaged in self-employment or employed as unpaid family workers. There was a decline in this proportion during the 1980s; yet in 1990, approximately 61 per cent of the male workforce and 69 per cent of the female workforce were in the informal sector. Since the capacity of the formal sector to create adequate job opportunities to meet the demands of an increasing workforce is still limited, the informal sector continues to be the main livelihood for the majority of the workforce with less educational attainment. The urban informal sector absorbs workers from rural areas who migrate temporarily to cities during slack cultivation periods. The informal sector also provides women with more freedom to combine income-earning activities with household chores. Nevertheless, since informal employment is less rewarding than formal employment, women are in a disadvantaged position, and the substantial increase in the number of employed women has not necessarily been followed by an equal increase in their economic welfare.

Several studies have shown that a large number of jobs in the informal sector are

Table 43. Percentage distribution of employed persons aged 10 years and over by employment status and sex: 1980 and 1990

Employment status	1980		1990	
	Male	Female	Male	Female
Formal sector	31.9	23.9	39.2	31.1
Employer	2.1	1.1	1.8	0.9
Employee	29.8	22.8	37.4	30.2
Informal sector	66.5	74.4	60.7	68.5
Self-employed	28.0	21.7	21.0	16.3
Self-employed assisted by family member/temporary help	11.8	23.3	28.4	16.7
Unpaid family worker	11.8	29.4	11.3	35.5
Status not stated	1.6	1.7	0.2	0.4
Total	100.0	100.0	100.0	100.0

Source: Central Bureau of Statistics, population censuses of 1980 and 1990.

temporary, part-time and unpaid, and that most workers, especially women, have multiple occupations. It is also important to make a distinction between earning workers as opposed to unpaid family workers. The proportion of the employed persons engaged as unpaid family workers is considerably higher among females than among males. In 1990, for instance, unpaid family workers constituted about 35 per cent of all female workers and 52 per cent of the female workers in the informal sector, the corresponding proportions among males being about 11 and 19 per cent respectively.

There was also a substantial increase in the number of unpaid family workers during the 1980s, and this increase was more pronounced among females than among males. Between 1980 and 1990, the number of female unpaid family workers increased by 4.1 million, or 84.3 per cent, compared with an increase by only 1.1 million, or 27.3 per cent, in the number of male unpaid family workers. Consequently, the share of females in total unpaid family workers increased from 54.6 per cent in 1980 to 64.7 per cent in 1990. Further, while the proportion of unpaid family workers among all female workers increased by 6 percentage points from 29.4 to 35.5 per cent, that among males decreased by 0.5 percentage points, from 11.8 to 11.3 per cent. Thus, although women have only recently been successful in breaking the household barrier to enter the labour market, not all of the female job-seekers succeeded in finding suitable paid jobs and had therefore to settle for non-paying jobs in family enterprises.

The amount of formal sector employment – employers or paid employees – had increased very significantly during the 1980s, from 11.0 million to 18.1 million, or by 64 per cent, for males and from 4.0 million to 7.9 million, or by 99.0 per cent, for females. Consequently, the proportionate share of formal sector workers increased from 31.9 to 39.2 per cent in the case of males and from 23.9 to 31.1 per cent in the case of females (annex table E.7 and table 43). The striking increase in women's participation in the formal sector has been referred to by several researchers as the feminization of the formal sector.

Within the formal sector, the vast majority (about 97 per cent of females and 95 per cent of males) are paid employees. There was also a considerable increase in the number of paid employees between 1980 and 1990, and again this increase was more pronounced for females than for males. The number of female paid employees more than doubled, from about 3.8 million to 7.9 million, compared with an increase by 68 per cent in male paid employees from 11.0 million to 18.1 million. The dramatic expansion in the number of female paid employees was due to two important factors: the rising level of educational attainment of women, qualifying them for employment in the formal sector; and the increase in the number of formal sector employment opportunities for women resulting from the structural transformation of the economy. However, available job opportunities in the formal sector are concentrated in and around major urban areas.

The employment status of the employed workforce also differs between urban and rural areas of the country. According to the 1990 census data, the majority of employed males and females in the urban areas are in the formal sector, and the majority in the rural areas are in the informal sector. Although there is no urban/rural difference in the proportions engaged as employers, the proportions reported as paid employees in urban areas are more than double those reported for rural areas in respect of both males and females (table 44). This is largely because the majority of formal sector paid jobs are concentrated in urban areas.

In regard to informal sector participation, the 1990 census data showed that while the majority of male or female urban informal workers were in self-employment, in the rural areas the majority of males were in self-employment, while the females were largely employed as unpaid family workers. These workers constituted about 43 per cent of all female workers in rural areas compared with only 12 per cent in urban areas (table 44). Available evidence indicates that modernization and commercialization of agriculture have tended to reduce women's paid employment, while increasing their unpaid labour inputs on family farms. For

Table 44. Percentage distribution of employed persons aged 10 years and over by employment status, residence and sex: 1990

Employment status	Indonesia		Urban		Rural	
	Male	Female	Male	Female	Male	Female
Formal sector	39	31	64	58	30	23
Employer	2	1	2	1	2	1
Employee	37	30	62	57	28	22
Informal sector	61	69	36	42	70	77
Self-employed	21	16	20	18	21	16
Self-employed assisted by family member/temporary help	29	17	13	12	35	18
Unpaid family worker	11	36	3	12	14	43
Total	100	100	100	100	100	100

Source: Central Bureau of Statistics, *Population of Indonesia: Results of the 1990 Population Census.*

instance, current agricultural practices such as direct planting and increased use of weedicides are seriously displacing large numbers of women because transplanting and weeding have traditionally been the work of women. Further, with increasing emphasis on larger-scale, export-oriented industries, there has been a stagnation in many traditional manufacturing industries which are more labour-intensive and have been employing a larger proportion of women, especially during slack periods of the agricultural cycle.

(d) Hours worked

Since a very substantial proportion of all working women are engaged in part-time jobs, the average number of hours worked by women is significantly lower than that of men. Available data show that in 1991, for instance, women worked on an average 42 hours per week compared with 45 hours by men. But this male-female differential varied across the several industrial sectors, being more marked in the agriculture, mining and trade sectors, where men worked seven to nine hours longer than women. It was only in the public service sector that females worked longer hours than males (table 45).

(e) Wages and earnings

Although there was a significant rise in women's labour-force participation during the 1980s, and women have started moving into the

formal sector in increasing numbers, discrimination against female employees remains a major problem in Indonesia. The gender-biased discrimination in employment is often expressed through differential terms and conditions of employment.

Available studies indicate that more female than male workers are employed on a temporary (limited-term contracts or no contracts) or casual (hired informally) basis as part of the putting system. For instance, a 1992 study of women workers in the garment and food and tobacco processing industries in Surabaya and Sidoarjo reported that the proportion of workers paid on a monthly basis was only 23 per cent among females compared with 40 per cent among males. This study also found that instead of hiring regular full-time workers and entering into written work contracts with them, specifying wage and non-wage entitlements as well as providing security of and protection in employment, employers resorted to hiring workers on a non-regular basis in accordance with business fluctuations. This hiring practice results in substantial savings to the employers because temporary, daily-rated and piece workers are not entitled to non-wage benefits.

As a result of the differences in hiring practices and terms and conditions of employment, there are substantial differentials in the average earnings of male and female workers. Available data indicate that, on an average,

57

Table 45. Average number of hours worked per week by main industrial sector and sex: 1989 and 1991

Industrial sector	1989			1991		
	Male	Female	Difference male/female	Male	Female	Difference male/female
Agriculture, forestry, hunting and fishing	40	30	10	39	30	9
Mining and quarrying	45	35	10	44	36	8
Manufacturing industry	47	44	3	48	45	3
Electricity, gas and water	45	31	14	45	41	4
Construction	48	50	−2	49	46	3
Wholesale and retail trade, restaurants and hotels	52	53	−1	52	50	2
Transport, storage and communications	53	45	8	53	46	7
Finance, insurance, real estate and business services	46	45	1	46	44	2
Public services	41	45	−4	41	46	−5
Other	45	23	22	38	32	6
All sectors	44	41	3	45	42	3

Source: Central Bureau of Statistics, *Labourers/Employees Situation in Indonesia,* 1989 and 1991.

women's earnings are 50-70 per cent of men's earnings. Even when educational attainment is the same, women are paid far less than men. This sex differential in earnings is greatest among workers with the least formal education; in 1990, the average monthly earnings of males with less than primary education was Rp 61,699, or slightly more than double the female earnings of Rp 30,149. Even among academy or university graduates (tertiary education), males earn about 32 per cent more than their female counterparts (table 46).

It is also evident from table 46 that between 1986 and 1990, there was a decrease in women's earnings relative to those of men for all educational categories except for those with upper secondary education. Table 46 also shows

that the higher the level of educational attainment, the greater the earnings index, this index being higher for females than for males. For instance, in 1990 the average earnings of a worker with tertiary education compared with those of a worker with less than primary education were nearly five times in the case of females and a little over three times in the case of males. This would mean that higher educational attainment enables women to earn higher income.

The substantial differences in wages or earnings between male and female workers could be attributed to several factors. In the first place, males have, on the average, been longer in the labour force than females, and wages of seniors are usually higher than those

Table 46. Average monthly earnings by level of educational attainment and sex: 1986 and 1990

Level of educational attainment	Average monthly earnings (rupiahs)				Female/male earning ratio		Earnings index (less than primary = 100)			
	1986		1990				Male		Female	
	Male	Female	Male	Female	1986	1990	1986	1990	1986	1990
Less than primary	44 657	22 740	61 699	30 149	51	49	100	100	100	100
Primary completed	58 361	29 638	69 333	34 970	51	50	131	124	130	116
Lower secondary	82 652	50 743	115 809	61 920	61	53	185	188	223	205
Upper secondary	103 850	71 648	137 732	101 194	69	74	233	223	315	336
Tertiary	167 064	117 762	260 227	177 800	70	68	374	322	518	490

Source: Central Bureau of Statistics, *Social Indicators on Women in Indonesia,* 1991 and 1992.

of juniors. Second, the higher educational attainment and skill level of male workers enable them to secure higher-paid jobs. Third, as noted earlier, male workers work longer hours than female workers and hence receive higher remuneration. Fourth, there is also discrimination against women on grounds of sex alone; while married male workers are entitled to family allowances, married female workers are not entitled to such benefits.

Available data also indicate that wages of female workers are different from those of male workers even within the same sector (table 47). In 1991, for instance, earnings of female workers were significantly lower than those of males in all sectors except the transport sector, in which female earnings were substantially higher than those of males. Women's earnings are also among the lowest in the agricultural sector, about half the earnings of males, although about half the female labour force is in that sector. A 1993 study by the International Labour Organization (ILO) found that the wage differential in the agricultural sector was related to the high degree of gender-based division of labour in that sector. It should also be noted that women's earnings in agriculture often include a substantial component paid in kind, particularly in the form of a share of the harvested crop. This is often one of the most

important sources of family income for rural households, despite the fact that it is highly seasonal.

5. Unemployed labour force

Data from the 1980 and 1990 population censuses indicate that the unemployment ratio among females aged 10 years and over was higher than that among males in rural as well as urban areas and that there was an increase in these rates between 1980 and 1990. The overall female unemployment rate increased from 2.2 to 2.6 per cent in rural areas and from 3.0 to 7.6 per cent in urban areas during the 1980s. Thus, unemployment rates are considerably higher among urban females compared with their rural counterparts; in 1990, the urban female overall unemployment rate of 7.4 per cent was nearly three times the rate of 2.7 per cent reported in respect of rural females (table 48).

Unemployment rates varied considerably by age. In 1990, unemployment among the youngest age groups 10-14 and 15-19 years was highest among urban males, but the rate was higher for females in the ages 20-34 years, with little difference among older workers. There was also a sharp increase in male as well as female unemployment rates at ages 10-14 years in urban and rural areas between 1980 and 1990.

6. Access to credit

Although a number of governmental and non-governmental programmes offer small-scale credit to both men and women, gender-disaggregated data relating to formal credit markets are extremely scarce. Nevertheless, available data and information suggest that women participate actively in the rural financial sector, accounting for an estimated 20-30 per cent of the borrowers in government-sponsored small-credit schemes, about 55-60 per cent in non-banking financial institutions, and around 80 per cent in government pawnshops (see table 49).

A 1988 World Bank study reported that women engaging in income-earning activities generally have smaller incomes and hence the loans required by them are smaller than those

Table 47. Average earnings of female workers as a proportion of average earnings of male workers by main industrial sector: 1989, 1990 and 1991

Major industrial sector	Female/male earning ratio		
	1989	1990	1991
Agriculture	54.4	51.2	54.5
Mining	44.8	46.8	80.4
Manufacturing	53.5	46.5	58.2
Electricity	73.0	74.6	67.3
Construction	91.6	103.6	100.4
Trade	67.0	62.9	73.8
Transport	112.2	144.6	135.1
Finance and business services	70.5	77.0	88.3
Public services	63.4	64.2	63.4
Others	54.9	57.3	45.8
All sectors	57.0	56.0	61.2

Source: Central Bureau of Statistics.

Table 48. Unemployment rates by age group and sex: 1980 and 1990

Age group	1980				1990			
	Urban		Rural		Urban		Rural	
	Male	Famale	Male	Famale	Male	Famale	Male	Famale
10-14	5.8	4.7	2.3	3.7	22.3	15.1	6.7	7.3
15-19	8.2	5.7	2.6	3.7	18.2	14.7	5.4	7.3
20-24	6.7	6.5	1.8	2.9	15.4	16.6	4.1	5.8
25-29	2.3	2.6	0.9	2.0	5.5	7.2	1.2	2.1
30-34	1.0	1.5	0.6	1.7	1.8	2.6	0.5	1.1
35-44	0.8	1.0	0.5	1.5	0.1	1.5	0.3	0.9
45+	1.0	0.8	0.5	1.3	1.1	1.0	0.4	0.8
All ages 10+	2.7	3.0	1.0	2.1	5.4	7.4	1.7	2.7

Source: Central Bureau of Statistics, cited in International Labour Organization, *A Comprehensive Women's Employment Strategy for Indonesia,* final report of an ILO/United Nations Development Programme mission, 1993.

required by men. The 1993 ILO study referred to earlier also found that across the seven provincial governments' financial institutions, the average size of loans granted to women was only US$ 59, as compared with US$ 87 for men. The time constraints due to household responsibilities, and the "transaction costs" associated with borrowing, such as having to travel to larger urban centres to obtain a loan, and paper work expenses, are important factors limiting women's demand for formal credit. Collateral for loans also tends to be a problem, especially if land titles are required, since these are most often in the name of the (male) head of household. Women's assets such as jewellery, batik and animals are seldom acceptable as collateral for loans in the formal sector.

Village-level studies indicate that women also borrow from informal sources such as suppliers, traders, neighbours, moneylenders etc. at extremely high rates of interest. In the informal sector, the use of credit for productive purposes is often mixed with credit for consumption, especially in poor households. Women may save for (or invest their profits in) children's education or emergencies such as family illnesses.

Many of the small-scale credit programmes for women employ group models, where credit is dispensed by the implementing agency to a group rather than to individuals. Such womens' groups operate in the farming and informal sectors, and tend to have excellent repayment records which are much better than those of comparable male groups. Funds are often administered by the group, and loans to other members depend on the repayments from those taking the first loans.

The General Rural Credit Scheme (KUPEDES) operates at the subdistrict level through the village sub-branches of the government-owned commercial bank, Bank Rakyat Indonesia. Loans range from Rp 25,000 to Rp 25 million for virtually any productive purpose. Repayment schedules for working capital are three to nine months, with a grace period. Single payments range from 3 to 12 months. The interest rate is 2 per cent per month, with 0.5 per cent refunded for payment on time. Borrowers' applications must be signed by the village head and the borrower's spouse. Collateral must cover the value of the loan and should be in the form of land, buildings, vehicles or other property. Women's participation is between 25 and 35 per cent (table 49).

Women's participation is higher, around 60 per cent, in the district credit bodies (BKKs), which provide small, short-term, unsecured loans and accept savings deposits from the rural poor in Central Java. BKKs are locally administered and local officials assist in evaluating borrowers. The signature of the village headman is required for loans over Rp 25,000, but approval is not required for smaller loans. BKK-type institutions operate in East Java, West Sumatera, and West Java.

Table 49. Women's participation in credit programmes and institutions: 1988

Credit programme/ institutions	Percentage of loans granted to women	Average amount of loan (rupiahs)	Collateral required	Effective monthly rate of interest (percentage)	Level of operation
Pawn shop	80	5 000	Yes	3.0-4.0	District
District credit body Central Java	80	55 000	No	2.0-4.8	Sub-district/ village
Enterprise credit	57	. .	No	3.3	Vilage
Bank Pasar, Denpasar[a]	29	736 000	Yes	2.5-3.0	Provincial city
KUPEDES (BRI Unit Desa) (General rural credit scheme)	25 per cent loans to women 75 per cent of co-signers women	330 000	Yes	1.7-2.6	Sub-district
State and private banks[b]	23.4 (transport, 30.8; other services, 30.5)	5 000	Yes	3.0-4.0	Regency

Source: World Bank, *Indonesia: Rural Sector Credit Review* (1988).

[a] Largely urban clientele.
[b] Mostly urban lending.
Two dots (. .) indicate that data are not available.

Other schemes include those operated through Village Cooperative United. Its major programme for poor women is Kredit Candak Kulak (KCK), which provides small loans of Rp 5,000 to Rp 50,000 without collateral or security. Women appear to constitute the majority of borrowers in this programme. The Family Welfare Movement (PKK) (see sect. F.4 below) also provides small loans to women, but these seem to be mostly for consumption purposes.

A programme specifically for women is the Programme to Increase the Role of Women in Small Industries. This programme, which is administered by the Department of Industry, is intended for women aged 16-60 years who are in regular economic activity and are heads of households, economically weak, or are high school drop-outs. This programme involves 120 cooperative enterprise groups in 24 provinces. Funds are provided by Bank Indonesia, with the United Nations Development Programme (UNDP) providing collateral. The programme is coordinated by the State Ministry for the Role of Women.

The National Family Planning and Coordi-nation Board provides loans to family planning acceptors and other women of childbearing age as an incentive for family planning. Loans of Rp 500,000 to Rp 1,500,000 are provided as start-up capital to members of selected groups, of whom at least 55 per cent should be family planning acceptors. Repayments to the Board are used to establish programmes in other villages.

F. WOMEN IN PUBLIC LIFE

1. Women in politics

For centuries, Indonesian women have participated actively in politics and civic life, facing little of the rigid and formalized discrimination to which women are subjected in many other countries. Their political participation grew together with their participation in the indepen-dence movement in the early part of this century. Women began to organize themselves and worked hand in hand with other organiza-tions and political movements towards achieving national independence. The first Indonesian Women's Congress, which took place in 1928, served as the first common and open expression of women's commitment to Indonesia's indepen-dence and political participation at the national level. These historical and cultural facts of women's status and role had facilitated the enactment of laws and formulation of policies, providing for a favourable legal and policy environment for the participation of women in the decision-making process at the national, provincial and local levels.

As noted in the introduction, the basic rights of men and women are guaranteed in the Indonesian Constitution of 1945. Article 27 of the Constitution stipulates that all citizens shall have equal status before the law and in government. More specifically, equal political rights for women were ensured in 1961, when Indonesia ratified the United Nations Convention on the Political Rights of Women, giving them the right to vote, stand for election and hold public office. Furthermore, Election Law No. 15/1969 underlined the equal rights of all eligible citizens to vote and stand for election. Consequent on these developments, Indonesian women have exercised their civic and political rights by participating actively in the general elections since 1955 and holding public office.

Available data indicate that the proportion of eligible women exercising their voting rights had increased from 60 per cent in 1955 to more than 80 per cent during the 1971 and 1977 general elections and further to 90 per cent at the 1992 elections. Since the electoral system is based on proportional representation and a list system, the representation of political groups or parties in the House of Representatives will be commensurate with the number of votes collected by them at the general elections. The very high female voter turnout has thus enabled women to play a decisive role in the election of the political groups that would form the government.

Despite the fact that a very high percentage of women voters have exercised their franchise at various elections, women's representation in the key decision-making bodies at the national level is quite low. Although the number and relative share of women in the membership of Parliament and in the People's Consultative Assembly has increased since 1971, in 1993 women accounted for only 12.4 per cent of the total parliamentarians and 7.6 per cent of the total members of the People's Consultative Assembly (table 50).

Although the relative share of women in national-level legislative bodies is quite low, available evidence indicates that there has been an improvement in the quality of the women members of these bodies. The higher educational levels of women politicians and their increased political awareness indicate their enhanced capacity to represent women's interests. For instance, women members of parliament have initiated a programme to raise the level of awareness of women's needs and issues among parliamentarians, particularly women parliamentarians. In 1993, for the first time, a group of women intellectuals involved in women's graduate studies at the University of Indonesia were invited for a dialogue with 25 female and a smaller number of male parliamentarians. The dialogue focused on the importance of women's status and roles in development and the need to incorporate women's special needs in policy-making.

Table 50. Participation of females in parliamentary assemblies: 1971-1993

Election years	Parliament			People's Consultative Assembly		
	Total members	Female members	Percentage female	Total members	Female members	Percentage female
1971	460	31	6.7	920	51	5.5
1977	460	37	8.0	920	58	6.3
1982	460	42	9.1	920	69	7.5
1987	500	57	11.4	1 000	104	10.4
1992	500	59	11.8	1 000	101	10.1
1993	500	62	12.4	500	38	7.6

Source: Government of Indonesia.

The fourth and fifth development Cabinets, appointed in 1982 and 1987 respectively, included two women ministers, the Minister of State for the Role of Women, and the Minister of Social Affairs. Several women members of the House of Representatives have been elected as either chairperson or vice-chairperson of three of the 11 Committees, while the Committee for Inter-Parliamentary Cooperation also has a woman as chairperson and as one of the vice-chairpersons.

The overall representation of women in provincial legislative bodies is also rather low, and remained constant at 12 per cent of total membership between 1987 and 1992. However, this proportion varies markedly across the 27 provinces, and in 1992 ranged from a low of 7 per cent in Aceh, South Sumatera and Lampung to 18 per cent in Central, North and South Sulawesi, East Timor and East Nusa Tenggara, and to a very high 22 per cent in Maluku. Between 1987 and 1992, the relative share of women members increased in 10 provinces, decreased in 6 and remained constant in 11 provinces (annex table F.1).

Women's participation in decision-making at the highest levels is also relatively limited. In 1992, women constituted 12.5 per cent of the members of the Supreme Court, only 5.1 per cent of the members of the Supreme Advisory Council, and 2.0 per cent of the members of the State Audit Board. While there was an increase in the proportionate share of women is the Supreme Court to 14.9 per cent and in the Supreme Advisory Council to 6.5 per

cent in 1993, there were no women members in the State Audit Board (table 51).

2. Women in the civil service

An encouraging trend in the government or civil service during the past two decades has been the increase in female employees in both absolute and relative terms. Available data indicate that the proportion of females in the total number of civil servants had increased steadily, from 18 per cent in 1974 to 27 per cent in 1984, and further to 34 per cent in 1993. More women have been employed as civil servants since the implementation of the law on compulsory government service for all graduates of medical, dental and pharmacy schools, as well as some public academies. Graduates from these institutions are required to work for the government for a minimum of three years immediately after graduation.

Data for selected years from 1984 to 1993 show that the proportionate share of female employees had increased steadily over these years in all government departments except the Education Department, in which this proportion increased up to 1992 but declined sharply thereafter. The relative share of female employees also varied markedly between the 21 departments, from a low of 8.2 per cent in the Forestry Department to about 20-25 per cent in the Departments of Justice, Transmigration, Industry, Labour, Trade, Cooperatives and Post and Telecommunications, and to more than 33 per cent in the Departments of Education

Table 51. Female participation in the highest decision-making bodies: 1990, 1992 and 1993

Decision-making body	1990			1992			1993		
	Membership			Membership			Membership		
	Both sexes	Female	Percent-age female	Both sexes	Female	Percent-age female	Both sexes	Female	Percent-age female
Supreme Court	56	7	12.5	56	7	12.5	47	7	14.9
Supreme Advisory Council	39	2	5.1	39	2	5.1	46	3	6.5
State Audit Board	300	6	2.0	300	6	2.0	300	..	..

Source: Office of the State Minister for the Role of Women.

Two dots (. .) indicate that data are not available.

and Social Services, and further to more than half (54.2 per cent) in the Department of Health. Generally, women tend to be employed in larger numbers in those departments dealing with social welfare and social development (annex table F.2).

Although, as noted earlier, the proportionate share of females in the civil or government service has almost doubled during the past two decades, in 1993 females still constituted a smaller proportion of employees at the lowest or unskilled level (13.2 per cent) and in the highest salary level (12.2 per cent), while they accounted for about 40 and 32 per cent of employees at grades II and III respectively. Between 1984 and 1993, there was an increase in women's share of positions at all levels or grades, but this was more pronounced at level III, rising from 19.3 per cent in 1984 to 31.8 per cent in 1993 (table 52).

Data from the State Civil Service Administration Board also show that female representation in structural or decision-making positions, referred to as "echelon" occupations, is comparatively very small. There are five echelons in the Indonesian civil service system, and the total number of positions in all these echelons constitute only about 8 per cent of the total number of civil service posts. It will be noted from annex table F.3 that the share of women in echelon occupations increased slightly, from 12 per cent in 1987 to 13 per cent in 1992, and that they accounted for 14 per cent of the positions at the lowest level (Echelon V) and 11 per cent at the highest level (Echelon I),

but only 5 and 7 per cent respectively at levels II and III.

Although, as noted earlier, 43 per cent of all employees in the Department of Education were female, in 1992 only 24 per cent of the school principals were women. In 1992, women also accounted for 26 per cent of the senior researcher positions and 29 per cent of the assistant researcher positions in the national government. Among the four professional occupations in the civil service reported by the State Civil Service Administration Board, women constituted 60 per cent of the paramedics and 45 per cent of the medical doctors in 1992, while they accounted for 24 per cent of the judges and 19 per cent of the attorneys (annex table F.3).

Office-holding by women at the higher levels of the civil administration is as yet not common in Indonesia. The highest position currently held by a woman is that of Regent, and in 1991, women accounted for only 927, or 1.4 per cent, of the 66,371 village heads in the country. The proportion of female village heads was highest in Central and East Java (3 and 2 per cent respectively) while there were no women village heads in Jakarta.

3. Women in diplomatic service

Available data indicate that there is gross under-representation of women in the Indonesian diplomatic or foreign service. In recent years, the number of women in the regular intakes of candidates for professional

Table 52. Percentage of female civil servants in national government by rank: selected years, 1984-1993

Rank	1984	1987	1990	1992	1993
Golongan I	12.3	12.5	12.8	13.0	13.2
Golongan II	35.0	37.5	38.9	39.4	39.9
Golongan III	19.5	24.5	26.8	27.3	31.8
Golongan IV	8.9	10.2	10.9	11.0	12.2

Source: State Civil Service Administration Board.

Note: "Golongan" refers to a grade which is determined by qualifications, length of service, and certain promotion criteria.

diplomatic training in the Department of Foreign Affairs has fluctuated between 8 and 25 per year. It was only in 1991/92 that 26 per cent (25 of the 98) of persons recruited for training were women. In 1993/94, women constituted 16.7 per cent of the trainee intakes (table 53).

Table 53. Professional diplomatic training intakes, by sex: 1990/91-1993/94

Year	Both sexes	Female	Percentage female
1990/91	45	8	17.8
1991/92	98	25	25.5
1992/93	73	11	15.1
1993/94	48	8	16.7

Source: Ministry of Foreign Affairs.

In 1985, there was only one woman among the 64 ambassadors and, although the number of women ambassadors has risen since then, in 1994 there were only 4 women among the 76 ambassadors, constituting about 5 per cent of the ambassador cadre. The appointment of women as consul-general or consul is even very low; in 1994, there was only one woman among the 24 positions of consul general/consul. Women are also very poorly represented among the general staff servicing the country's diplomatic missions abroad. Although there has been a more than doubling in the number of females posted to the general staff of missions, from 31 in 1985 to 75 in 1994, women accounted for only 8.0 per cent of the 860 persons serving in the general staff of the diplomatic missions abroad (table 54).

4. Women in social and community development

Non-governmental organizations as well as government agencies dealing with women's affairs have encouraged women to involve themselves actively in village community resilience bodies and social organizations. These organizations serve as an important forum for women to develop their ability to conduct fruitful negotiations and formulate and implement programmes to meet the felt needs of people at the grassroots levels. The State Ministry for the Role of Women and various women's organizations conduct management and leadership programmes specifically designed for women at the provincial and district levels.

Women's organizations, whose 25 million members are spread out in urban and rural areas, have engaged in extensive development activities, in terms of both advocacy and actual implementation of programmes. Although there are 94 women NGOs in the country, only four of them are considered major ones in view of

Table 54. Female participation in diplomatic missions by level: selected years, 1985-1994

Year/sex		Ambassadors	Consul-general	Consul	Chargé d'affaires	General staff
1985	Both sexes	64	9	12	4	693
	Female	1	..	..	..	31
	Percentage female	1.6	–	–	–	4.5
1990	Both sexes	67	11	11	3	710
	Female	2	1	..	..	62
	Percentage female	3.0	9.0	–	–	8.7
1992	Both sexes	70	12	11	4	871
	Female	3	..	1	..	67
	Percentage female	4.3	–	9.0	–	7.7
1994	Both sexes	76	17	7	2	935
	Female	4	1	..	..	75
	Percentage female	5.3	5.9	–	–	8.0

Source: Ministry of Foreign Affairs.

Two dots (. .) indicate that data are not available.

their large membership. The Indonesian Women's Congress (KOWANI), established in 1928, serves as an umbrella organization for several professional, religious and other women's groups, and represents an estimated 20 million women through its member organizations. The Congress maintains formal relationship with all major government agencies and participates in the national policy formulation process, including the Broad Guidelines of State Policies.

Dharma Wanita, established in 1974, is an association of the wives of civil servants, and is organized into units and sub-units that correspond to the agencies and departments of the government ministries. The Department of Education accounts for the largest share, about 1.1 million or 43 per cent of the total membership of Dharma Wanita. An important objective of the association is to encourage its members to engage in activities outside their homes. It participates actively in government-sponsored and government-supported programmes such as family planning, income-generating activities, functional literacy programmes, health and nutrition, environment and cooperatives.

The third major women's organization is Dharma Pertiwi, an umbrella organization comprising the five organizations for wives of armed forces and police personnel: Persit Kartika Chandra Kirana (Army); Jalasenastri (Navy); PIA Ardhya Garini (Air Force); Bhayangkari (Police); and Itakan Kesejahteraan Keluarga ABRI, or Armed Forces Family Welfare League. Dharma Pertiwi is also actively engaged in educational social welfare programmes which are primarily intended for its members.

The Family Welfare Movement (PKK) is a community-based movement for villages and neighbourhoods. It was started in 1964 with women's group activities in communities in Central Java, and was subsequently extended to other provinces. It came to be officially recognized as a national movement in 1972. An estimated two million PKK volunteers are currently involved in village development programmes, concentrated in 10 areas: comprehension and practical application of *Pancasila* (the State philosophy); mutual self-help; food production; garment-making; housing and household maintenance; education and skill training; health; development of cooperatives; protection and conservation of the environment; and appropriate domestic planning. PKK programmes are funded from the development and recurrent budgets of the national, provincial and local governments.

Although PKK does not have a registered membership and is technically a non-governmental organization, it operates under the aegis of the Ministry of Home Affairs. At the national level, the PKK Motivating Team is chaired by the wife of the Home Minister, while the wife of the Governor chairs the Team at the provincial level. At the village level, PKK forms one section of the Village Community Resilience Body, with the chairperson of the village PKK motivating team also serving as the vice-chairperson of the Village Community Resilience Body. Since 1993/94, each PKK at the village level has been receiving a grant of Rp 900,000 annually in Presidential Aid.

The smaller NGOs, including religious organizations, are concerned with specific issues relating to women, such as domestic violence, child abuse and harassment of women workers. Generally, they are community-based and have limited financial resources; yet they play an increasingly important role, particularly in areas such as family planning and safe motherhood.

Indonesian women are also active in a number of professional associations. For instance, the number of women in the Indonesian Journalists Association increased from 106, or 5 per cent, in 1983-1987 to 238, or 7 per cent, in 1992. In the Indonesian Publishers Association, females account for about 16 per cent of the total number of registered general director and director publishers; while the number of female members in the Board of the Association increased from 3 in 1985-1988 to 12 in 1988-1993. In 1993, women constituted about 41 per cent of the members of the Film Artists Association. In the private sector, women decision makers are playing an increasing role in the manufacturing and service sectors. Women are also represented in the Indonesian Chambers of Commerce.

PART II
ANNEX TABLES

Table B.1 Area, population, population density and population growth rate by province

Province	Area (sq km)	Population (thousands) 1990	Density 1990	Growth 1980-1990
Aceh	55 392	3 417	61.7	2.7
North Sumatera	70 787	10 254	144.9	2.1
West Sumatera	49 778	4 001	80.4	1.6
Riau	94 561	3 283	34.7	4.2
Jambi	44 800	2 016	45.0	3.4
South Sumatera	103 688	6 278	60.5	3.1
Bengkulu	21 168	1 181	55.8	4.4
Lampung	33 307	6 006	180.3	2.6
Jakarta	590	8 225	13 940.7	2.4
West Java	46 300	35 380	764.1	2.6
Central Java	34 206	28 519	833.7	1.2
Yogyakarta	3 169	2 915	919.8	0.6
East Java	47 921	32 490	678.0	1.1
Bali	5 561	2 779	499.7	1.2
West Nusa Tenggara	20 177	3 371	167.1	2.2
East Nusa Tenggara	47 876	3 270	68.3	1.8
East Timor	14 874	750	50.4	3.1
West Kalimantan	146 760	3 237	22.1	2.7
Central Kalimantan	152 600	1 398	9.2	3.9
South Kalimantan	37 660	2 599	69.0	2.3
East Kalimantan	202 440	1 877	9.3	4.4
North Sulawesi	19 023	2 480	130.4	1.6
Central Sulawesi	69 726	1 705	24.5	2.8
South Sulawesi	72 781	6 983	95.9	1.4
South-East Sulawesi	27 686	1 351	48.8	3.7
Maluku	74 505	1 853	24.9	2.8
Irian Jaya	421 981	1 631	3.9	3.3
Indonesia	1 919 317	179 249	93.4	2.0

Source: Central Bureau of Statistics.

Table C.1 Enumerated population by age group and sex: censuses of 1980 and 1990

Age group	1980 census			1990 census		
	Both sexes	Male	Female	Both sexes	Male	Female
0-4	21 049 945	10 760 699	10 289 246	20 985 144	10 760 859	10 224 285
5-9	21 267 168	10 838 280	10 428 888	23 223 058	11 928 095	11 294 963
10-14	17 688 924	9 180 469	8 508 455	21 482 141	11 044 127	10 438 014
15-19	15 427 986	7 600 408	7 827 578	18 926 983	9 520 440	9 406 543
20-24	12 902 969	5 936 512	6 966 457	16 128 362	7 583 305	8 545 057
25-29	11 234 730	5 576 315	5 658 415	15 623 530	7 457 150	8 166 380
30-34	8 090 022	3 964 125	4 125 897	13 245 794	6 584 325	6 661 469
35-39	8 466 657	4 130 274	4 336 383	11 184 217	5 788 441	5 395 776
40-44	7 421 747	3 677 987	3 743 760	8 081 635	4 010 254	4 071 381
45-49	6 165 142	3 014 986	3 150 156	7 565 664	3 723 922	3 841 742
50-54	5 426 318	2 699 966	2 726 352	6 687 586	3 289 190	3 398 396
55-59	3 413 029	1 727 762	1 685 267	4 831 697	2 321 621	2 510 076
60-64	3 278 116	1 567 860	1 710 256	4 526 451	2 219 069	2 307 382
65-69	1 764 291	846 637	917 654	2 749 724	1 329 162	1 420 562
70-74	1 572 234	695 054	877 180	2 029 026	945 876	1 083 150
75+	1 576 490	716 930	859 560	1 972 356	867 636	1 104 720
Not stated	30 705	17 406	13 299	4 415	2 205	2 210
All ages	146 776 473	72 951 670	73 824 803	179 247 783	89 375 677	89 872 106

Source: Central Bureau of Statistics, *Population of Indonesia: Results of the Sub-sample of the 1980 Population Census;* and *Results of the 1990 Population Census.*

Table C.2 Sex ratio by province and residence: 1980 and 1990

Province	Indonesia		Urban		Rural	
	1980	**1990**	**1980**	**1990**	**1980**	**1990**
Aceh	101.5	101.1	111.6	106.0	100.5	100.2
North Sumatera	100.7	99.8	101.3	99.7	100.5	99.8
West Sumatera	95.5	95.9	102.3	97.3	94.6	95.5
Riau	104.0	105.2	106.8	107.0	103.0	104.3
Jambi	105.7	104.3	107.8	104.5	105.3	104.3
South Sumatera	102.0	101.2	103.1	100.8	101.7	101.3
Bengkulu	103.2	105.6	108.1	107.5	102.7	105.2
Lampung	107.3	105.5	105.3	103.3	107.6	105.8
Jakarta	102.6	101.9	102.5	101.9	104.5	–
West Java	99.1	100.5	100.6	100.9	98.7	100.3
Central Java	96.6	97.5	95.7	96.2	96.8	97.9
Yogyakarta	96.2	96.7	101.0	98.3	94.9	95.4
East Java	95.5	96.0	94.8	95.0	95.7	96.3
Bali	98.4	99.5	101.3	100.7	97.9	99.0
West Nusa Tenggara	98.3	95.5	102.3	98.9	97.7	94.8
East Nusa Tenggara	99.6	98.3	125.7	111.7	97.7	96.7
East Timor	–	107.2	–	122.7	–	106.0
West Kalimantan	103.5	103.8	105.3	103.5	103.1	103.9
Central Kalimantan	106.3	106.6	108.5	105.4	106.1	106.9
South Kalimantan	98.8	99.6	102.2	101.2	97.9	99.0
East Kalimantan	111.6	110.9	111.1	109.9	112.0	111.9
North Sulawesi	102.3	102.7	100.3	98.3	102.7	104.1
Central Sulawesi	106.4	105.1	108.2	102.9	106.3	105.5
South Sulawesi	94.9	95.5	98.7	97.3	94.1	94.9
South-East Sulawesi	96.9	99.7	105.3	102.3	96.1	99.2
Maluku	104.4	103.8	108.1	104.5	104.0	103.7
Irian Jaya	109.3	110.5	123.9	121.0	105.6	107.3
Sumatera	102.0	101.5	103.5	101.6	101.6	101.5
Java	97.4	98.3	98.6	98.7	97.0	98.1
Bali and Nusatenggara	98.8	98.3	106.5	103.0	97.7	97.4
Kalimantan	103.8	104.4	106.4	105.3	103.1	104.1
Sulawesi	97.9	98.6	100.0	98.5	97.6	98.7
Maluku and Irian Jaya	106.5	106.9	117.4	112.9	104.7	105.3
Indonesia	98.8	99.4	100.2	99.8	98.4	99.3

Sources: Central Bureau of Statistics, *Population of Indonesia: Results of the 1980 Population Census;* and *Results of the 1990 Population Census.*

70

Table C.3 Percentage distribution of the enumerated population by age group, sex and residence: censuses of 1980 and 1990

Age group	Indonesia				Urban areas				Rural areas			
	1980		1990		1980		1990		1980		1990	
	Male	Fe-male	Male	Fe-male	Male	Fe-male	Male	Fe-male	Male	Fe-male	Male	Fe-male
0-4	14.8	13.9	12.0	11.4	14.1	13.4	10.9	10.2	15.0	14.2	12.6	11.9
5-9	14.9	14.1	13.3	12.6	13.2	12.6	12.1	11.5	15.3	14.5	13.9	13.1
10-14	12.6	11.5	12.4	11.6	12.1	11.8	11.6	11.2	12.7	11.4	12.7	11.8
15-19	10.4	10.6	10.7	10.4	12.2	12.9	11.7	12.5	9.8	9.8	10.2	9.6
20-24	8.1	9.4	8.4	9.5	10.6	11.0	10.7	11.4	7.5	9.1	7.5	8.7
25-29	7.5	7.7	8.3	9.1	8.6	8.2	9.5	9.8	7.4	7.6	7.8	8.7
30-34	5.4	5.6	7.4	7.4	5.8	5.7	8.0	7.8	5.4	5.6	7.1	7.2
35-39	5.7	5.9	6.5	6.0	5.6	5.6	6.6	5.9	5.8	6.0	6.4	6.0
40-44	5.0	5.1	4.5	4.5	4.8	4.7	4.4	4.2	5.0	5.2	4.5	4.7
45-49	4.1	4.3	4.2	4.3	3.6	3.9	3.9	3.9	4.3	4.4	4.3	4.4
50-54	3.7	3.7	3.7	3.8	3.3	3.3	3.3	3.4	3.8	3.7	3.8	3.9
55-59	2.4	2.3	2.6	2.8	2.2	2.1	2.3	2.5	2.4	2.3	2.7	2.9
60-64	2.1	2.3	2.4	2.6	1.7	1.9	2.1	2.2	2.3	2.4	2.7	2.7
65-69	1.2	1.2	1.5	1.6	0.9	1.1	1.3	1.4	1.2	1.3	1.6	1.7
70-74	1.0	1.2	1.1	1.2	0.7	0.9	0.8	1.0	1.0	1.2	1.2	1.3
75+	1.0	1.2	1.0	1.2	0.7	1.0	0.7	1.0	1.0	1.2	1.1	1.3
All ages	100.0	100.0	100.0	100.0	100.0	100.0	100.0	100.0	100.0	100.0	100.0	100.0

Source: Central Bureau of Statistics, *Population of Indonesia: Results of the Sub-sample of the 1980 Population Census;* and *Results of the 1990 Population Census.*

Table C.4 Numerical distribution of population aged 10 years and over by level of educational attainment and gender: censuses of 1980 and 1990

Educational attainment	1980 census			1990 census		
	Both sexes	Male	Female	Both sexes	Male	Female
Never attended	42 369 086	22 256 844	20 112 242	21 952 791	7 084 886	14 867 905
Incomplete primary	..	..	..	42 480 415	21 188 599	21 291 816
Primary	22 176 315	12 384 554	9 791 761	40 996 434	21 192 895	19 803 539
Junior high: General	5 150 036	3 044 213	2 105 823	13 392 558	7 393 433	5 999 125
: Vocational	1 149811	725 922	423 889	1 088 539	654 599	433 940
Senior high: General	2 166813	1 457 075	709 738	7 882 905	4 790 499	3 092 406
: Vocational	2 344 382	1 503 371	841 011	5 204 538	3 045 822	2 158 716
Diploma	315 629	228 905	86 724	352 505	204 194	148 311
Academy/diploma	..	..	..	700 801	443 022	257 779
University	229 628	178 252	51 376	986 699	688 123	298 576
Not stated	54 409	25 146	29 263	1 396	651	745
Total	75 956 109	41 804 282	34 151 827	135 039 581	66 686 723	68 352 858

Source: Central Bureau of Statistics.

Two dots (. .) indicate that data are not available.

Table C.5 Literacy rates of the population aged 10 years and over by sex and province: 1990 census

(Percentage)

Province	Both sexes	Male	Female	Male/female difference
Aceh	87.3	92.0	82.7	9.3
North Sumatera	92.4	95.7	89.2	6.5
West Sumatera	91.3	94.3	88.6	5.7
Riau	90.1	94.1	86.0	8.1
Jambi	89.5	94.2	84.6	9.6
South Sumatera	90.7	94.5	86.8	7.7
Bengkulu	89.0	93.5	84.3	9.2
Lampung	89.5	93.5	85.4	8.1
Jakarta	96.1	98.1	94.0	4.1
West Java	87.3	91.9	82.7	9.2
Central Java	81.2	88.5	74.3	14.2
Yogyakarta	79.9	88.4	71.8	16.6
East Java	77.3	85.0	70.0	15
Bali	76.4	84.4	68.6	15.8
West Nusa Tenggara	69.6	77.9	62.0	15.9
East Nusa Tenggara	78.1	82.3	74.1	8.2
East Timor	45.1	52.8	36.8	16
West Kalimantan	77.3	84.9	69.4	15.5
Central Kalimantan	90.9	94.2	87.4	6.8
South Kalimantan	89.8	93.7	85.9	7.8
East Kalimantan	89.8	93.5	85.7	7.8
North Sulawesi	95.3	95.9	94.8	1.1
Central Sulawesi	89.1	91.8	86.2	5.6
South Sulawesi	77.8	81.8	74.1	7.7
South-East Sulawesi	82.4	88.5	76.4	12.1
Maluku	92.6	94.9	90.2	4.7
Irian Jaya	68.7	74.8	62.0	12.8
Indonesia	84.1	89.6	78.7	10.9

Source: Central Bureau of Statistics, *Population of Indonesia: Results of the 1990 Population Census.*

Table C.6 Infant mortality rate per thousand live births by sex and province: 1980 and 1990

Province	1980 census			1990 census		
	Both sexes	Male	Female	Both sexes	Male	Female
Aceh	93	99	82	58	65	52
North Sumatera	89	97	81	61	68	54
West Sumatera	121	132	112	74	82	67
Riau	110	123	103	65	72	58
Jambi	121	130	110	74	81	66
South Sumatera	102	106	89	71	79	64
Bengkulu	111	116	97	69	77	62
Lampung	99	106	89	69	77	62
Jakarta	82	89	73	40	46	35
West Java	134	141	120	90	99	82
Central Java	99	106	89	65	72	58
Yogyakarta	62	70	56	42	47	36
East Java	97	109	91	64	71	57
Bali	92	98	81	51	58	45
West Nusa Tenggara	189	202	173	145	157	133
East Nusa Tenggara	128	135	114	77	85	70
East Timor	..	..	..	85	93	77
West Kalimantan	119	127	107	81	89	74
Central Kalimantan	100	109	91	58	64	51
South Kalimantan	123	132	100	91	99	83
East Kalimantan	100	109	91	58	65	52
North Sulawesi	93	104	87	63	70	56
Central Sulawesi	130	139	118	92	101	84
South Sulawesi	111	117	98	70	78	63
South-East Sulawesi	116	127	107	77	85	70
Maluku	123	135	115	76	84	69
Irian Jaya	105	117	98	80	88	73
Indonesia	109	117	98	71	79	64

Source: Central Bureau of Statistics, *Social Indicators on Women in Indonesia, 1987 and 1992.*

Two dots (. .) indicate that data are not available.

Table C.7 Life expectancy at birth by province and sex: 1980, 1990 and 1994

Province	1980		1990		1994	
	Male	Female	Male	Female	Male	Female
Aceh	54.2	57.5	60.8	64.5	63.3	67.2
North Sumatera	54.4	57.7	60.3	63.9	62.3	66.2
West Sumatera	48.3	51.2	57.5	60.9	61.4	65.2
Riau	49.0	53.0	59.4	63.0	62.8	66.7
Jambi	48.8	51.7	57.6	61.3	61.6	65.3
South Sumatera	52.8	56.0	58.1	61.6	60.6	64.4
Bengkulu	51.1	54.2	58.5	62.0	61.9	65.7
Lampung	52.8	56.0	58.5	62.0	60.9	64.7
Jakarta	56.0	59.5	64.3	68.2	67.3	71.3
West Java	46.9	49.7	54.2	57.4	58.4	62.1
Central Java	52.8	56.0	59.4	63.0	62.0	65.8
Yogyakarta	58.9	63.5	64.7	68.5	65.9	69.8
East Java	52.3	55.5	59.7	63.3	62.3	66.1
Bali	54.4	57.7	62.5	66.2	65.2	69.1
West Nusa Tenggara	38.0	40.7	44.6	47.3	51.2	54.3
East Nusa Tenggara	47.8	50.7	56.9	60.3	61.3	65.1
East Timor	..	..	55.3	58.6	60.8	63.7
West Kalimantan	49.2	52.2	56.0	59.4	59.4	63.1
Central Kalimantan	52.3	55.5	61.0	64.7	64.0	67.9
South Kalimantan	48.3	51.3	54.1	57.3	57.3	60.9
East Kalimantan	52.3	55.5	60.8	64.5	63.8	67.7
North Sulawesi	53.2	56.5	59.8	63.4	62.1	65.9
Central Sulawesi	47.1	50.0	53.8	57.0	57.6	61.2
South Sulawesi	50.9	54.0	58.3	61.8	61.6	65.3
South-East Sulawesi	49.2	52.2	56.8	60.2	60.2	63.9
Maluku	47.8	50.7	57.0	60.4	61.0	64.8
Irian Jaya	50.9	54.0	56.2	59.6	58.4	62.0
Indonesia	50.9	54.0	58.1	61.5	61.2	64.9

Source: Central Bureau of Statistics.

Two dots (. .) indicate that data are not available.

Table D.1 Percentage distribution of household heads by sex, province and residence: 1994

Province	Province		Urban		Rural	
	Male	Female	Male	Female	Male	Female
Aceh	84.7	15.3	86.7	13.3	84.3	15.7
North Sumatera	87.9	12.1	87.4	12.6	88.2	11.8
West Sumatera	80.1	19.9	79.6	20.4	80.3	19.7
Riau	90.4	9.6	92.0	8.0	89.7	10.3
Jambi	91.3	8.7	92.4	7.6	91.0	9.0
South Sumatera	91.1	8.9	88.8	11.2	92.1	7.9
Bengkulu	91.5	8.5	91.1	8.9	91.7	8.3
Lampung	92.4	7.6	88.2	11.8	93.2	6.8
Jakarta	88.3	11.7	88.3	11.7	–	–
West Java	88.0	12.0	87.6	12.4	88.2	11.8
Central Java	86.6	13.4	84.9	15.1	87.3	12.7
Yogyakarta	80.8	19.2	78.0	22.0	84.9	15.1
East Java	84.6	15.4	83.5	16.5	85.0	15.0
Bali	91.9	8.1	88.6	11.4	93.5	6.5
West Nusa Tenggara	85.9	14.1	87.1	12.9	85.7	14.3
East Nusa Tenggara	89.7	10.3	86.4	13.6	90.1	9.9
East Timor	91.3	8.7	90.4	9.6	91.4	8.6
West Kalimantan	92.6	7.4	90.5	9.5	93.1	6.9
Central Kalimantan	92.8	7.2	91.9	8.1	93.0	7.0
South Kalimantan	86.2	13.8	87.2	12.8	85.8	14.2
East Kalimantan	93.6	6.4	92.0	8.0	95.1	4.9
North Sulawesi	89.6	10.4	87.1	12.9	90.4	9.6
Central Sulawesi	92.1	7.9	91.8	8.2	92.2	7.8
South Sulawesi	85.8	14.2	85.2	14.8	86.0	14.0
South-East Sulawesi	88.0	12.0	88.1	11.9	88.0	12.0
Maluku	91.0	9.0	86.8	13.2	92.3	7.7
Irian Jaya	94.6	5.4	94.3	5.7	94.7	5.3
Indonesia	87.4	12.6	86.5	13.5	87.9	12.1

Source: Central Bureau of Statistics, *National Socio-economic Survey (SUSENAS), 1994.*

Table D.2 Percentage of ever-married women aged 10 years and over marrying for the first time at ages 10-16 and 17-18, by province: 1980, 1990 and 1994

Province	1980 census		1990 census		1994 DHS	
	Age at first marriage (years)					
	10-16	17-18	10-16	17-18	10-16	17-18
Aceh	35.3	29.9	28.1	28.5	16.5	32.4
North Sumatera	24.1	25.7	20.4	23.3	9.4	21.3
West Sumatera	38.3	27.5	30.8	25.4	24.5	30.3
Riau	38.1	25.9	29.0	25.2	14.9	25.6
Jambi	46.0	26.1	39.4	26.0	25.5	30.3
South Sumatera	31.0	28.2	29.4	26.2	17.8	29.2
Bengkulu	32.8	28.1	29.7	26.5	19.0	28.4
Lampung	45.5	26.9	36.8	26.4	23.0	30.1
Jakarta	37.1	21.7	28.1	20.7	14.5	22.4
West Java	58.8	22.5	50.8	25.1	38.5	31.3
Central Java	45.3	26.5	39.1	27.2	28.4	31.3
Yogyakarta	23.7	26.2	19.5	24.0	13.2	24.9
East Java	51.4	24.0	44.7	25.2	37.2	31.7
Bali	16.4	23.7	14.7	21.3	4.8	18.8
West Nusa Tenggara	21.4	27.2	18.7	27.5	12.9	26.4
East Nusa Tenggara	11.9	19.7	9.2	18.2	3.8	14.5
East Timor	..	..	..	..	8.3	20.5
West Kalimantan	26.9	26.2	25.5	25.7	15.4	29.7
Central Kalimantan	32.5	26.3	29.2	25.6	15.0	31.5
South Kalimantan	48.3	24.2	41.9	24.2	32.2	30.8
East Kalimantan	34.1	25.8	32.9	24.4	25.7	27.2
North Sulawesi	13.5	22.0	12.9	20.6	9.0	20.3
Central Sulawesi	26.5	25.8	26.0	24.9	18.2	28.4
South Sulawesi	31.0	24.8	24.4	25.3	17.1	27.4
South-East Sulawesi	25.3	27.8	20.9	28.4	12.7	27.4
Maluku	16.5	19.3	15.0	21.4	7.2	19.2
Irian Jaya	22.4	20.5	25.8	23.6	15.3	30.2
Indonesia	43.4	24.6	37.0	25.1	26.9	29.1

Sources: Central Bureau of Statistics, population censuses of 1980 and 1990; and *Indonesia Demographic and Health Survey, 1994.*

Two dots (. .) indicate that data are not available.

Table D.3 Percentage of ever-married women in Java aged 25-49 years who were married before 20 years of age, by background characteristics and current residence: 1991

Background characteristics	Current residence			
	Big city	Town	Rural	Total
Age group	56.0	66.0	80.4	70.0
25-29	52.1	64.5	78.2	67.2
30-34	54.2	60.7	76.7	65.8
35-39	52.8	64.4	81.4	68.5
40-44	59.9	76.6	85.0	75.4
45-49	68.3	76.6	83.6	78.2
Education				
No education	86.9	83.4	85.3	85.3
Some primary	83.1	81.3	82.9	82.7
Completed primary	71.5	75.1	82.4	77.6
Secondary	39.3	45.6	54.1	43.6
Academy/university	4.9	. .	. .	5.1
Religion				
Muslim	63.8	69.2	80.8	73.7
Protestant	22.8	48.6	71.8	35.6
Catholic	20.2	29.6	63.3	30.5
Others	21.0	. .	. .	19.0
Work status before marriage				
Worked	43.5	55.5	73.3	61.3
Not worked	66.8	78.6	89.1	79.2

Source: Rini Savitridina, "Determinants and consequences of early marriage in Java, Indonesia", *Asia-Pacific Population Journal,* vol. 12, No. 2, 1997.

Two dots (. .) indicate that data are not available.

Table D.4 Percentage distribution of currently married women aged 15-49 years by contraceptive method currently used and according to selected background characteristics: 1994

Background characteristics	Any method	Any modern method	Any traditional method	Not currently using	Total
Residence					
Urban	60.2	55.8	4.4	39.8	100.0
Rural	52.5	50.5	2.0	47.5	100.0
Region/residence					
Java-Bali	58.4	56.4	2.0	41.6	100.0
Urban	62.0	58.6	3.5	38.0	100.0
Rural	56.6	55.4	1.2	43.4	100.0
Outer Java-Bali I	49.5	45.5	4.0	50.5	100.0
Urban	55.8	48.1	7.7	44.2	100.0
Rural	47.8	44.8	3.0	52.2	100.0
Outer Java-Bali II	45.7	41.8	3.9	54.3	100.0
Urban	54.0	48.7	5.3	46.0	100.0
Rural	43.3	39.8	3.5	56.7	100.0
Education					
No education	39.6	38.1	1.5	60.4	100.0
Some primary	52.6	50.6	1.9	47.4	100.0
Completed primary	58.2	56.1	2.1	41.8	100.0
Some secondary	62.6	57.5	5.1	37.4	100.0
Number of living children					
0	9.0	8.9	0.1	91.0	100.0
1	54.1	52.1	2.0	45.9	100.0
2	65.2	61.8	3.3	34.8	100.0
3	65.4	62.3	3.1	34.6	100.0
4+	53.3	50.2	3.1	46.7	100.0
Total	54.7	52.1	2.7	45.3	100.0

Source: Central Bureau of Statistics and others, *Indonesia Demographic and Health Survey, 1994.*

Table D.5 Percentage of currently married women who want no more children, by number of living children and selected background characteristics: 1994

Background characteristic	0	1	2	3	4	5	6+	Total
	\multicolumn{7}{c	}{Number of living children[a]}		Total
Residence								
Urban	2.5	6.5	54.7	79.6	88.3	91.7	94.4	56.1
Rural	3.2	8.1	50.0	67.2	78.1	83.6	83.8	49.7
Region/residence								
Java-Bali	3.5	8.5	58.7	78.6	86.6	89.7	89.4	53.3
Urban	2.7	6.6	58.3	81.4	89.4	93.2	97.3	56.7
Rural	3.8	9.3	58.9	77.1	84.9	87.9	85.5	51.6
Outer Java-Bali I	2.0	5.5	34.8	58.4	74.9	82.1	83.5	49.0
Urban	2.1	6.2	43.0	74.4	88.1	87.5	89.0	55.4
Rural	2.0	5.3	32.3	54.5	71.0	80.7	82.3	47.2
Outer Java-Bali II	1.6	6.0	36.0	57.2	71.9	80.5	83.7	47.3
Urban	1.2	6.8	46.3	73.9	79.0	92.1	88.3	52.5
Rural	1.7	5.7	32.8	51.9	69.9	77.8	82.9	45.8
Education								
No education	10.0	18.5	51.6	70.0	79.2	83.4	82.2	59.6
Some primary	5.3	11.6	48.5	65.6	77.4	85.5	88.0	56.9
Completed primary	0.8	5.9	52.2	72.3	83.1	85.8	85.3	46.3
Some secondary	0.1	3.8	53.3	77.7	88.1	90.2	92.6	45.8
Total	3.0	7.6	51.4	70.9	81.3	85.8	86.5	51.5

Source: Central Bureau of Statistics and others, *Indonesia Demographic and Health Survey, 1994.*

Note: Women who have been sterilized are considered to want no more children.

[a] Including current pregnancy.

Table E.1 Numerical distribution of the population aged 10 years and over by type of activity and gender: 1980 and 1990

Activity status	1980 census			1990 census		
	Both sexes	Male	Female	Both sexes	Male	Female
Economically active	52 109 926	34 999 320	17 110 606	73 913 704	47 397 836	26 515 868
Working	51 191 512	34 486 029	16 705 483	71 569 971	46 083 672	25 486 299
Looking for work	918 414	513 291	405 123	2 343 733	1 314 164	1 029 569
Not economically active	52 343 702	16 350 271	35 993 431	61 125 877	19 288 887	41 836 990
Attending school	19 029 302	10 494 517	8 534 785	25 775 383	13 609 414	12 165 969
Housekeeping	22 447 450	598 566	21 848 884	25 442 038	596 785	24 845 253
Other	10 866 950	5 257 188	5 609 762	9 908 456	5 082 688	4 825 768
Total	104 453 628	51 349 591	53 104 037	135 039 581	66 686 723	68 352 858

Sources: Central Bureau of Statistics, *Population of Indonesia: Results of the 1980 Population Census;* and *Results of the 1990 Population Census.*

Table E.2 Numerical distribution and percentage increase of economically active persons aged 10 years and over by age group and sex: 1980 and 1990

Age group	Male		Female		Percentage increase: 1980-1990	
	1980	1990	1980	1990	Male	Female
10-14	1 159 175	1 313 643	810 485	923 297	13.3	13.9
15-19	3 615 568	4 534 425	2 436 949	3 163 121	25.4	29.8
20-24	4 709 893	6 088 638	2 314 700	3 715 083	28.8	60.5
25-290	5 143 557	7 032 717	2 041 535	3 730 200	36.7	82.7
30-34	3 769 906	6 424 851	1 587 817	3 226 916	70.4	103.2
35-39	3 949 376	5 672 087	1 832 523	2 773 541	43.6	51.4
40-44	3 492 582	3 929 817	1 687 382	2 174 187	12.5	28.8
45-49	2 829 529	3 603 317	1 453 810	2 069 519	27.3	42.4
50-54	2 423 252	3 099 499	1 219 143	1 753 450	27.9	43.8
55-59	1 465 758	2 047 259	676 486	1 207 526	39.7	78.5
60-64	1 207 214	1 786 621	547 762	929 154	48.0	69.6
65+	1 225 820	1 864 075	498 948	849 515	52.1	70.3
Not stated	7 690	887	3 066	359	–	–
Total	34 999 320	47 397 836	17 110 606	26 515 868	35.4	55.0

Source: Central Bureau of Statistics.

Table E.3 Labour-force participation rates of persons aged 10 years and over by level of educational attainment, residence and sex: 1980 and 1990

(Percentage)

Residence/educational attainment level	1980			1990		
	Both sexes	Male	Female	Both sexes	Male	Female
Indonesia						
No schooling	54	81	40	58	84	46
Some primary	46	62	28	48	62	34
Primary	52	70	28	57	75	38
Lower secondary	41	59	20	47	63	27
Upper secondary	67	77	46	69	82	51
Academy	81	88	59	84	91	73
University	87	94	67	88	93	75
Urban						
No schooling	43	72	33	45	72	35
Some primary	34	48	20	36	48	25
Primary	41	60	19	46	64	29
Lower secondary	38	55	16	41	57	23
Upper secondary	61	73	40	65	78	47
Academy	80	88	59	83	91	69
University	88	94	69	88	93	77
Rural						
No schooling	55	82	41	61	85	48
Some primary	49	65	30	52	65	37
Primary	56	74	33	62	79	42
Lower secondary	50	64	25	54	69	33
Upper secondary	76	84	57	78	88	59
Academy	84	91	61	88	93	78
University	84	92	56	87	93	70

Source: Central Bureau of Statistics, population censuses of 1980 and 1990.

Table E.4 Percentage distribution of the labour force by marital status, sex and residence: 1990

Age group/ residence	Not married		Married		Divorced		Widowed		All statuses	
	Male	Female	Male	Female	Male	Female	Male	Female	Male	Female
Urban										
10-14	99.3	99.8	0.6	0.1	0.0	0.0	0.0	0.0	100.0	100.0
15-19	98.6	90.7	1.4	8.6	0.0	0.6	0.0	0.1	100.0	100.0
20-24	83.2	53.0	16.3	44.2	0.5	2.4	0.1	0.4	100.0	100.0
25-29	43.2	19.5	55.9	76.0	0.7	3.8	0.2	0.7	100.0	100.0
30-34	14.7	7.2	83.9	87.2	1.1	4.0	0.3	1.6	100.0	100.0
35-39	7.1	4.6	91.1	87.2	1.4	4.4	0.4	3.8	100.0	100.0
40-44	5.2	3.3	92.4	84.3	1.4	4.4	1.0	8.0	100.0	100.0
45-49	4.2	2.7	93.0	78.9	1.5	4.9	1.3	13.5	100.0	100.0
50-54	3.9	1.9	92.1	68.5	1.5	5.1	2.4	24.4	100.0	100.0
55-59	3.7	1.6	90.2	60.3	1.8	4.6	4.3	33.5	100.0	100.0
60-64	3.9	1.5	88.2	45.3	1.7	4.7	6.2	48.5	100.0	100.0
65+	7.3	4.1	76.7	27.6	1.8	3.5	14.2	64.7	100.0	100.0
All ages 10+	50.0	40.3	48.0	48.7	0.8	2.8	1.2	8.2	100.0	100.0
Rural										
10-14	99.0	99.4	0.9	0.5	0.1	0.0	0.1	0.0	100.0	100.0
15-19	96.9	76.2	2.9	22.2	0.2	1.5	0.0	0.1	100.0	100.0
20-24	64.8	25.9	33.5	69.8	1.6	3.9	0.2	0.4	100.0	100.0
25-29	22.2	7.1	75.4	87.9	2.1	3.9	0.3	1.1	100.0	100.0
30-34	7.6	3.0	90.1	91.0	1.7	3.9	0.6	2.1	100.0	100.0
35-39	4.5	1.8	93.3	89.7	1.5	4.3	0.8	4.2	100.0	100.0
40-44	3.4	1.6	93.8	84.8	1.3	4.6	1.4	8.9	100.0	100.0
45-49	3.2	1.2	93.3	80.1	1.4	5.2	2.1	13.5	100.0	100.0
50-54	3.2	1.2	91.8	69.6	1.3	5.3	3.7	23.9	100.0	100.0
55-59	2.9	0.9	91.2	62.8	1.3	5.8	4.6	30.5	100.0	100.0
60-64	3.1	1.1	88.2	47.1	1.5	5.7	7.2	46.0	100.0	100.0
65+	5.1	2.6	78.8	28.0	2.1	4.0	14.1	65.4	100.0	100.0
All ages 10+	41.2	30.0	55.8	56.5	1.2	3.4	1.8	10.1	100.0	100.0

Source: Central Bureau of Statistics, 1990 population census.

Table E.5 Numerical distribution of the employed population aged 10 years and over by major industrial sector and sex: 1980 and 1990

Major industrial sector	1980		1990	
	Male	Female	Male	Female
Agriculture, forestry, hunting and fishing	19 270 214	8 770 248	23 285 781	12 461 666
Mining and quarrying	303 788	65 494	586 424	126 047
Manufacturing	2 520 260	1 840 397	4 518 823	3 658 606
Electricity, gas and water	74 143	10 541	129 780	10 484
Construction	1 523 641	49 501	2 858 699	68 326
Wholesale and retail trade, restaurants and hotels	3 469 961	3 141 436	5 460 833	5 079 482
Transport, storage and communications	1 443 115	24 656	2 573 378	44 680
Finance, insurance, real estate and business services	196 081	35 854	525 672	156 876
Social and personal services	5 280 678	2 458 591	5 848 076	3 496 915
Others	36 943	10 346	19 463	23 556
Industry not stated	367 205	298 419	276 743	359 661
Total	34 486 029	16 705 483	46 083 672	25 486 299

Source: Central Bureau of Statistics.

Table E.6 Numerical distribution of employed persons aged 10 years and over by broad occupational category and sex: 1980 and 1990

Broad occupational category	1980		1990	
	Male	Female	Male	Female
Professional, technical and related workers	1 000 499	541 881	1 501 059	1 129 093
Administrative and managerial workers	65 864	9 656	129 530	15 405
Clerical and related workers	1 649 881	258 402	2 775 550	754 308
Sales workers	3 485 193	3 121 014	5 291 792	4 918 013
Service workers	1 072 962	1 300 767	1 261 818	1 737 788
Agricultural workers	19 226 359	8 757 161	23 242 538	12 473 526
Production, transport equipment operators and related workers	7 226 998	2 382 279	11 665 759	4 144 319
Others	337 983	26 598	54 586	22 986
Occupation not stated	420 290	307 725	161 040	290 861
Total	34 486 029	16 705 483	46 083 672	25 486 299

Source: Central Bureau of Statistics.

Table E.7 Numerical distribution of employed persons aged 10 years and over by employment status and sex: 1980 and 1990

Employment status	1980		1990	
	Male	Female	Male	Female
Formal sector				
Employer	723 239	180 693	823 152	223 115
Employee	10 284 974	3 803 508	17 246 260	7 707 125
Total formal sector	11 008 213	3 984 201	18 069 412	7 930 240
Informal sector				
Self-employed	9 666 373	3 619 067	9 667 459	4 145 196
Self-employed assisted by family member/temporary help	9 222 508	3 884 370	13 081 029	4 257 304
Unpaid family worker	4 077 154	4 909 752	5 188 747	9 048 988
Total informal sector	22 966 035	12 413 189	27 937 235	17 451 488
Status not stated	511 781	308 093	77 025	104 571
Total	34 486 029	16 705 483	46 083 672	25 486 299

Source: Central Bureau of Statistics.

**Table F.1 Percentage of women in total membership of provincial legislative bodies:
1987 and 1992**

Province	1987	1992	Change
Aceh	7	7	–
North Sumatera	13	14	+1
West Sumatera	16	9	–7
Riau	9	9	–
Jambi	13	16	+3
Bengkulu	9	11	+2
South Sumatera	7	7	–
Lampung	9	7	–2
Jakarta	10	11	+1
West Java	12	16	+4
Central Java	17	14	–3
Yogyakarta	11	11	–
East Java	14	9	–5
West Kalimantan	9	9	–
Central Kalimantan	9	9	–
East Kalimantan	20	9	–11
South Kalimantan	11	11	–
Bali	11	11	–
West Nusa Tenggara	11	11	–
East Nusa Tenggara	11	18	+7
East Timor	16	18	+2
South Sulawesi	13	18	+5
Central Sulawesi	16	13	–3
North Sulawesi	11	18	+7
South-East Sulawesi	18	18	–
Maluku	11	22	+11
Irian Jaya	11	11	–
All provinces	12	12	–

Source: Central Bureau of Statistics, *Social Indicators on Women in Indonesia,* 1989 and 1992.

Table F.2 Percentage of female civil servants by department: selected years, 1984-1993

Department	1984	1986	1990	1992	1993
Home affairs	10.9	12.8	16.2	16.8	17.7
Foreign affairs	14.5	15.8	17.8	18.7	19.0
Defence	19.0	20.0	24.3	25.2	27.8
Justice	16.3	17.6	19.0	20.0	19.7
Information	20.5	22.6	24.9	25.4	26.1
Finance	11.9	12.4	14.4	14.6	15.6
Trade	18.8	19.5	21.5	21.8	22.5
Agriculture	12.1	12.9	15.7	16.5	17.1
Industry	16.5	18.1	19.2	19.4	20.7
Mining	8.5	9.3	12.0	12.6	13.6
Public works	7.7	8.2	10.1	10.4	10.7
Transport	–	5.1	6.1	6.5	11.2
Education	38.8	40.7	42.5	42.7	36.9
Health	45.6	46.8	51.0	52.6	54.2
Religion	22.1	22.9	25.3	25.9	27.1
Labour	17.6	18.8	20.3	20.7	21.2
Transmigration	–	–	19.7	20.0	20.3
Social affairs	28.1	29.2	31.5	33.7	34.7
Cooperatives	–	15.5	21.8	22.4	23.3
Forestry	–	7.7	7.6	7.9	8.2
Post and telecommunications	17.9	21.4	23.8	23.9	25.1

Sources: Martha G. Logsdon, "Women civil servants in Indonesia: some preliminary observations", *Prisma*, No. 37, 1985; and Central Bureau of Statistics, *Social Indicators on Women in Indonesia,* 1991, 1992 and 1993.

Table F.3 Percentage of female civil servants in various occupational categories: 1987 and 1992

Occupational category	Percentage female		Change 1987-1992
Education	45	46	+1
Professors (Guru Besar)	23	24	+1
Readers (Lektor Kepala/Madya/Muda)	21	27	+6
Instructors (Asisten Ahli/Madya)	30	30	–
School principals (Kepala Sekolah)	23	24	+1
Primary teachers	49	51	+2
Secondary teachers	42	43	+1
Religious teachers	36	37	+1
Research	22	24	+2
Senior researcher (Peneliti Utama/Madya/Muda)	25	26	+1
Researcher (Peneliti Madya/Muda)	18	21	+3
Associate researcher (Ajun Peneliti Madya/Muda)	18	21	+3
Assistant researcher (Asisten Peneliti Madya/Muda)	27	29	+2
Structural positions	12	13	+1
Echelon I	10	11	+1
Echelon II	4	5	+1
Echelon III	6	7	+1
Echelon IV	10	11	+1
Echelon V	13	14	+1
Attorneys	18	19	+1
Judges	22	24	+2
Paramedics	55	60	+5
Medical doctors	41	45	+4
Other	19	20	+1
Total	31	33	+2

Source: State Civil Service Administration Board.

REFERENCES

Bell, Robert R. (1979), *Marriage and Family Interaction*. Illinois: The Dorsey Press. fifth ed.

Central Bureau of Statistics (1983), *Population of Indonesia:* Serie S, No. 2, *Results of the 1980 Population Census* (Jakarta).

———— (1993), *The 1992 Labour Force Situation in Indonesia* (Jakarta).

———— (1993), *The 1992 Social Welfare* (Jakarta).

———— (1994), *Welfare Indicators, 1993* (Jakarta).

———— (1994), *Statistical Year Book of Indonesia, 1993* (Jakarta).

———— (1995), *Social Indicators on Indonesian Women, 1991* (Jakarta).

———— (1995), *National Socio-economic Survey (SUSENAS)* (Jakarta).

Central Bureau of Statistics, National Family Planning Coordinating Board, Ministry of Health and Demographic and Health Surveys Macro International Inc. (1992), *The 1991 Demographic and Health Survey* (Jakarta).

Central Bureau of Statistics, National Family Planning Coordinating Board and Institute for Resource Development/ Westinghouse (1989), *The 1987 National Contraceptive Prevalence Survey* (Jakarta).

Central Bureau of Statistics, National Family Planning Coordinating Board, Ministry of Health, and Macro International Inc. (1996) *Demographic and Health Survey, 1994* (Jakarta).

Central Bureau of Statistics, United Nations Childrens Fund (1994), *Social Indicators on Indonesian Women, 1993* (Jakarta).

Corner, Lorraine (1991), "East and West Nusa Tenggara: isolation and poverty", in Hal Hill, ed., *Unity and Diversity, Regional Economic Development in Indonesia Since 1970* (Oxford University Press).

Department of Information and Office of the Minister of State for the Role of Women (1989), *The Women of Indonesia* (Jakarta).

Gardiner, Peter (1994), *Social Performance Assessment Indicators for Indonesia,* a report submitted to the Asian Development Bank.

Government of Indonesia (1992), *Country Report: Indonesia,* prepared for the Fourth Asian and Pacific Population Conference, Bali, Indonesia, August 1992.

———— (1995), *Indonesian Country Report: Review of Implementation of the Nairobi Forward-looking Strategies for the Advancement of Women, 1985-1992.*

Insan Harapan Sejahtera (1993), *A Study of Women's Issues in Agricultural Transformation,* a report submitted to the World Bank.

Ismael, Isa (1979), "On Java, divorce ends many child marriages", in Mark Hutter (1986), *The Changing Family. Comparative Perspectives* (New York, Macmillan).

International Labour Organization (1993), *A Comprehensive Women's Employment Strategy for Indonesia,* final report of an ILO/United Nations Development Programme (UNDP) mission.

———— (1985), Agama-agama di Indonesia: Sejarah dan Perkembangannya (Religions in Indonesia: Their History and Development) in *Agama dan Tantangan Zaman. Pilihan Artikel Prisma, 1975-1984 (Religion and Its Challenge. Selected Articles in Prisma, 1975-1984),* Jakarta, LP3ES.

Lim, Lin Lean (1992), "Employment situation and training needs of women workers in garments and food/tobacco processing in Surabaya/Sidoarjo, Indonesia", a report submitted to UNDP/ILO as part of project preparation for the industrial skills development project.

Logsdon, Martha G. (1985), "Women civil servants in Indonesia: some preliminary observations", *Prisma*, No. 37.

McDonald, Peter and Edeng H. Abdurahman (1979), *Marriage and Divorce in West Java: An Example of the Effective Use of Marital Histories* (Institute of Demography, Faculty of Economics, University of Indonesia).

Oey-Gardiner, Mayling (1991), Wanita dan Pria Kepala Rumah Tangga (Women-Men Headed Households) in Oey-Gardiner, Mayling and Soedarti Surbakti, *Strategi Kehidupan Wanita Kepala Rumahtangga (Survival Strategy of Women-headed Households)* (Jakarta, Central Bureau of Statistics).

Oey-Gardiner, Mayling and Sudarti Surbakti (1991), *Strategi Kehidupan Wanita Kepala Rumahtangga (Survival Strategy of Women-headed Households)* (Jakarta, Central Bureau of Statistics).

Office of the Minister of State for the Role of Women, Republic of Indonesia (1989), *The Changing Role of Women with Special Emphasis on their Economic Role: Country Report on Indonesia* (Jakarta).

Santoso, Guritningsih, Meithy Djiwatampu, and Bernadette N. Setiadi (1990), *Indonesian Women's Participation in Human Resource Development Cooperation Activities* (Jakarta, Faculty of Psychology, University of Indonesia), paper prepared for the Canadian International Development Agency.

Savitridina, Rini (1997), "Determinants and consequences of early marriage in Java, Indonesia", *Asia-Pacific Population Journal*, vol. 12, No. 2.

Sciortino, Rosalia M.E. (1992), *Care-takers of Cure. A Study of Health Centre Nurses in Rural Central Java*, a published dissertation (Amsterdam, Jolly).

Selvaratnam S. (1988), "Population and status of women". *Asia-Pacific Population Journal*, vol. 3, No. 2.

Sigit, Hananto (1989), "Transformasi Tenaga Kerja di Indonesia Selama Pelita" (Labour's transformation in Indonesia during PELITA) in *Prisma*, No. 18.

Suleeman, Evelyn (1993) "Women's education in Indonesia", a report submitted to the Economic and Social Commission for Asia and the Pacific.

United Nations Children's Fund (1989), *Situation Analysis of Children and Women in Indonesia* (1988, revised 1989).

University of Indonesia (1987), "Kecenderungan Kawin Muda di Kalangan Remaja Desa Suatu Studi Deskriptif Analitis di Desa Nanggung" (A descriptive study of a tendency to get married at a young age among the rural youth in Nanggung Village (unpublished research report) (Jakarta, Faculty of Social and Political Science, University of Indonesia).

World Bank (1988), *Indonesia: Rural Sector Credit Review.*

———— (1990), *Indonesian Strategy for a Sustained Reduction in Poverty, a World Bank country study* (Washington D.C.).

———— (1991) "Indonesia: Employment and training foundations for industrialization in the 1990s", draft report No. 9350-IND (Washington D.C.).

———— (1992), *"Indonesian women in development. A strategy for continued progress"*, internal discussion paper (Report No. IDP-112).

———— (1994), *Indonesia Sustaining Development* (Washington D.C.).